For the love of a good girl
Carlos & Jasmine

By: Quonni

Dedications:

Let me start by saying thank you to my readers for taking your time out to read my book. I also want to thank my husband

Vincent for believing in me and Also thank you to Shvonne Latrice for taking the time out to give me a chance at my dream. Also to the staff that make our books possible. You guys are greatly appreciated. Thank you guys

Synopsis:

Carlos is a New York through breed. He was born and raised by the streets of New York. Carlos has been hustling all his life trying to make a dollar out of fifteen cents. When Carlos finally gets noticed by his plug to take on the roll as boss man. Carlos did not know all the trial that came with being the boss. The losses he had to take just to remain on top. Can Los handle the pressure, or will he fold? Jasmine is the woman who choose to ride with los on his journey to the top. Being the strong-minded girl, she is can she take Los lifestyle, or will the pressure make her fold. Jas knew it wouldn't be easy to be Los woman, but she refused to let anything, or anyone take her from her love. Take a ride with Los and Jas to see what obstacles will come up in the life of these two.

Chapter 1: Jasmine
Chapter 2: Carlos
Chapter 3: Shae
Chapter 4: Jasmine
Chapter 5: Carlos
Chapter 6: Jasmine
Chapter 7: Shae
Chapter 8: Carlos
Chapter 9: Jasmine
Chapter 10: Carlos
Chapter 11: Shae
Chapter 12: Devin

Chapter 13: Jas
Chapter 14: Los
Chapter 15: Shae
Chapter 16: Los
Chapter 17: Devin
Chapter 18: Jas
Chapter 19: Los
Chapter 20: Devin
Chapter 21: Jas
Chapter 22: Shae
Chapter 23: Shae
Chapter 24: Los
Chapter 25: Jas
Chapter 26: Shae
Chapter 27: Jas
Chapter 28: Los
Chapter 29: Shae
Chapter 30: Jas
Chapter 31: Los
Chapter 32: Dezire
Chapter 33: Los
Chapter 34: Dez
Chapter 35: Jas
Chapter 36: Los
Chapter 37: Jas
Chapter 38: Dez
Chapter 39: Devin
Chapter 40: Jas
Chapter 41: Los
Epilogue

Chapter 1

JASMINE

Let me start by introducing Jasmine. She was the oldest of three siblings. Jessica and Jennifer were her two little sisters. Jessica is twelve, and Jennifer is fifteen. They lived in public housing with their alcoholic mother Lisa. They all had the same father. His name is James Washington.

After Jessica turned three, he up, and left after he had an argument with the girl's mother. He never came back, and that was when Lisa started drinking. Jas doesn't call her mom she calls her Lisa. That is because she has not been a mother since James left. Lisa became an alcoholic who let all kinds of men just come in, and out like she didn't have three daughters.

Jas was eighteen. When she was nine years old her mother had a man over who decided to come in her room and molest her. This happened for two years until Lisa decided he was no longer what she wanted. Jas had nightmares every night since then. Jas had never told anyone except her best friends. Carlos Wise and Shae Dunn were the only two people who knew what happen to her. They have known each other since middle school and have been each other's backbones through everything.

Carlos was twenty-one, and Shae was twenty. Jas worked full time as a waitress outside of taking care of her sisters. They were born and raised in Queens, NY... southside Jamaica to be exact. Luckily for her their neighbor, Mrs. Carol, had always been a big help. After being molested at a young age, Jasmine knew her mother didn't pay attention to the company she kept. Jas set up a routine with Mrs. Carol, so after school or whenever Jas was at work, Mrs. Carol kept the girls until she got there to pick them up from her apartment. You would've thought that Lisa would worry about her two younger daughters not coming straight home from school. She probably didn't even notice.

She got to the point where she stopped putting groceries and the things her and the girls needed in their apartment. She left everything at Mrs. Carol's apartment, and when she picked up the girls, she would grab some things until the morning. Yes, it was a lot on her to be just eighteen, but she would do anything for her sisters. The last thing she wanted was a repeat of what happened to her. Her two sisters were her pride and joy. There was no way she was letting some perv take their innocence. Luckily for her, she was never penetrated, so she was still a virgin. That experience in life made her so cold hearted. Relationships were not her cup of tea. What could these niggas offer her? Not shit but some heartache! Could she deal with that? Jas had a hard life already for her to be so young. All she hoped was that she could make it better some way.

"Jess and Jenn get your butts up. Y'all got school this morning!" Jas yelled from her bedroom. This was their daily routine. Get the girls up and ready for school. She always ironed their clothes the night before. They both had pretty hair, so she always kept it braided. Jas got them situated first so that while they were eating breakfast, she could slip something on herself. When the girls bathed at night, she sat in the bathroom. They knew what had happened to Jas when she was younger, so they know why she was so overprotective. Jas vowed that when she decided to have kids, she would not live the way her mother had them living. She would be the mother she never had. Jas wanted a big family.

"Stop damn yelling in my fuckin' house! Damn! I'm trying to sleep!" Lisa yelled
from the next room. Jas rolled her eyes. For this to be her house, she sure didn't do shit; not clean, cook, take care of her children, or anything at all unless a man was there or on the way over.

Jennifer walked into Jas's room to inform her they were up and getting ready. Jenn was the quiet one, the book smart one who didn't like confrontation. She liked peace. Then you had Jess, the smart ass who had an attitude from hell and didn't care who it bothered.

"Jas, we up. We were just putting on our clothes," Jenn said.

"Okay. Hurry up so I can get y'all fed and out the door before I have to cuss this lady out today!" Jas said. Jenn replied with *okay* and went back to their room. Jas tried very hard to respect Lisa as much as she could, but one thing she didn't like was when Lisa came at her sisters in the wrong way when they hadn't done anything, especially Jenn. Jas continued to get ready and then checked her phone.

Shae: Hey chica, you up yet
Jas: Yes, Wth you up?
Shae: Headed home from a long night. Honey I got to tell you about my bomb ass night, you work tonight
Jas: Yeah girl, you know I need all the hours as possible. You still going to Disney world with us? I'm so ready to see the girls faces!
Shae: Yesssss me too and yeah, I'm going. I already got the money for it
Jas: Ok, let me get them off to school and I'll be down there.
Shae: Ok boo

The girls had been wanting to go to Disney World, and she vowed to herself that she would see it through for them. She was surprising them with the trip once school let out. Both the girls had A/B honor roll. They deserved it.

"Come eat, girls. Your bus will be here in thirty minutes!"

"Okay! Coming!" The girls went into the kitchen where they sat and ate their cereal.

"Thanks, Jas!" both girls said and headed to the door. Jas grabbed her pocketbook and headed out the door with them. She hated having to walk through these halls with her sisters. You saw all types of needles and crack pipes. You could even catch crackheads getting high in the stairwell. She did not take her sisters on those staircases. If the elevator was broken, they would just miss until it was fixed. She would leave them with Mrs. Carol. Before work, she would go and get the work they missed. Their routine had been the same for quite some years. They already knew once they got home from school to head over to Mrs. Carol's house until Jas came home. She let them know that under no circumstance were they to go home without her. Jas worked her ass off just to make sure her sisters were good.

Jas always tried to pay Mrs. Carol for keeping her sisters. She wouldn't accept any form of payment from Jas. Jas was thankful for Mrs. Carol. She didn't think she would be able to survive without her. Jas was eighteen and had never experienced life. She'd never had a boyfriend or a friend for that matter. Raising her sisters had been her entire life. Jas didn't regret it one bit, because she loved those girls. Between them and her besties, that was as normal as her life got. That was the closest thing to a family she had.

She always caught herself thinking what life would be if she had a real mother to raise her and her sisters. Would she be living a normal teenage life? Would she be out at clubs partying and drinking? Would she be enjoying life? Would life be different if James had stayed and taken them with him instead of leaving? There were so many questions that Jas would never get the answers to. Jas at times hated the life her and her sisters were handed. None of them deserved it. You think Lisa cared? Hell no. She was worried about what man was next on her hit list. The shit was sad to Jas.

Jas vowed to never be a mother like hers. She now knew the definition of having kids to keep a man. There must have been more to life than just drinking your life away. Lisa used to be so beautiful. She had a body like Mary J. Blige. Lisa was bad as hell. When James was around, she kept her hair and nails done. She was so loving and nurturing. Now, Jas didn't know who this lady was.

Chapter 2

CARLOS A.K.A LOS

"Mmmm… Damn, Los. Don't stop, baby," this bad ass red bone said.

"Throw that shit back, baby…" Los told her. Los was drilling the shit out of her pussy. That shit was wet and gushy. Shawty was throwing it back so good. Los had to pull out to keep from cumming. He put his dick at her wet center and entered her. He pushed her arch until her stomach was touching the bed. Los gave her long, deep strokes until he felt her muscles contract around his third leg. Los couldn't help himself. He came inside of her. Los was fucking her so hard that he didn't even know the condom broke on them. That didn't stop him. His dick was still hard as a rock. Los had stamina without drugs, but when he did pop a molly, he was like Iron Man.

He kept fucking the red bone with no mercy. Los was what you would call a street nigga, the most eligible bachelor that all the ladies wanted; sexy chocolate complexion, brown eyes, nice slim build, and a low-cut fade. He was every girl's dream, but because of Los's background, he didn't trust so easily. Relationships for him were out the question. He fucked them and kept it moving. Los was a revolving door. He'd been fucking bitches since he was nine years old. He wasn't in the market to cuff none of these hoes he was fucking. He had always been a rude ass savage.

The ladies loved his rudeness. His favorite saying was M.O.E, money over everything. He ate, slept, shitted the streets. That was his life for the past several years. He had to become a man early in age because of his environment.

Los grew up in the foster system, going from different homes where he was beat on and touched on. After a while, he ran from the system and learned as much as he could from the streets. He met Dionne at the age of ten. They lived in the streets together. One day they walked up on this man that was in a brand-new Maserati. It was black on black with peanut butter seats. They had been out all day begging for change. Carlos felt the man had money to spare because of the car he was in. Los walked up on the man.

"Excuse me. Do you got a couple of dollars so me and my homie can eat?" The man looked between the two and couldn't help but to feel sorry. He told them to stay right there. Dionne was scared and wanted to haul ass, thinking the man was going to' rat them out. Carlos knew better. A nigga driving a Maserati was in the dope game. He wasn't fucking with no police.

When the man came back out, he handed both two-foot-long subs, two bags of chips, and two waters. He asked them where they'd been staying. Carlos informed him in the alley. The man wasn't feeling that one bit. He told them to hop in. He took Los and Dionne to the bricks. When he got there, he headed in the office. He came out and led them to the building they would now call home.

He led them into the apartment. He told Los and Dionne his name was Devin. He told them he would supply them with everything to survive, but they would work for him to pay it off. Carlos didn't care what they had to do. He was just glad he had a place to lay his head.

Devin took them to the mall and balled out on some shoes and clothes for them. They then went to C-town to grocery shop. The next stop was to get furniture. After everything was put up in the house, Devin had one more stop for them. He took them to Metro PCS to get some cell phones. He programed his number into both phones. He told both boys to get some rest and hit him up the next day to start working. They boys were excited. They'd gotten a brand-new life in a matter of hours.

Walking back into the building, that was when Los met Jas and Shae. Dionne was smitten with Shae. Los thought Jasmine was cute, but he was more focused on getting some money in his pocket. No chick wanted a broke ass nigga. Jas and Shae spoke and kept walking. Ever since that day, they were inseparable. Dionne was the one to break Shae's virginity. After that, he played her to the left.

Los and Dionne worked for Devin for years. He was their mentor and provider until they started to hustle a few years later. The only person that could get Los to step away from the block was Jas. She is his weak spot. He had been secretly in love with her since the day he meet them in the building lobby. Jas just didn't see it, or maybe she did.

"Mmm, Los. Baby go harder… Uh, baby, don't stop… Uhhhh, I'm about to cum, baby. Damnnn."

"Go ahead, baby. Let it go… I'm a cum with you." Right when they were about to reach their peak, Los's phone rang. He knew who it was before seeing the caller ID. It was Jas. Fifty Cent and Nivea's "Best Friend" poured from his phone. Los jumped out the pussy so fast that he almost broke his ankle.

"What the hell, Los? I was about to cum… the fuck," the red bone said.

"Aye, yo. Shut the fuck up so I can answer my phone, and don't say shit." Los picked up right before Jas hung up. Even though Jas knew Los was a full hoe, he still never let her see him in action. He loved the way Jas looked at him like he was her savior.

"Yo. What's up, Jas?"

"Hey, Los. You still coming to Disney World with us?"

"Yeah. Why wouldn't I be? Unless you changed your mind about a nigga going!"

"No. I was checking. I'm headed to Shae's house to talk to her about the trip info. Are you going to meet me over there, or you busy?"

"Nah. I'm not busy. I'm on the way now."

"Okay. Later." Los would drop anything for Jas, even the slut bucket he'd just met less than forty-eight hours ago.

"Aye, you got to swerve. I got shit to do," Los said to the girl.

"Are you kidding me right fucking now? We were in the middle of fucking," the red bone said.

"Man, get out. Damn." Los walked to the bathroom to shower before heading over to Shae's house. He expected the girl to be gone by the time he got out. When Los got out the shower, the girl was still sitting there, fuming. Los pulled his gun out the drawer and told her by the time he was dressed, she'd better be the fuck out his crib. Shawty scrambled to get her things while mumbling things under her breath. Los didn't give a fuck long as she was gone.

He got dressed in an all-black Nike tracksuit, sprayed some Curve cologne on, and grabbed his keys. Los headed down to Shae's floor. All three friends resided in the same building, just different floors. Carlos went straight to the stairs.

The elevators in the projects were terrible. Carlos walked down three flights of steps. He wasn't worried, because he never left home without his Beretta. He got to Shae's door and knocked. Jas opened the door, and he couldn't help but smile at her. His best friend was so cute to him. He put her in the mind of Calvin off the House of Payne. He was so sexy to her. Unbeknownst to them both, they were feeling the same way, but Jas refused to get caught up on her hoeish best friend.

While the two just stood there and daydreamed about each other, Shae shook her head. She could tell the attraction between the two, but neither would act on it. They were in love and didn't even know it. They had been in love since the playground days, but due to their backgrounds, both were scared to love. One thing Carlos did know was that Jas would be the one he married. She would be the one to bear his kids. She was the only girl that could make him get a funny feeling in the pit of his stomach.

Chapter 3

SHAE

Shae decided to clear her throat to let the two love bugs know that she was still standing there. They both looked at her in embarrassment. Shae didn't want them to hook up. Then she would feel like the third wheel. Most people said Shae looked like Nia Long but just a little thicker. Her personality was out of this world. She was extremely confident. Men found her irresistible, so she used them and abused them. Nothing in this world was free.

"So back to the task at hand. How long we staying at Disney World? How many rooms we getting? Do I need a date?" Shae asked.

"Dang. Slow down, Shae. Too many questions at once," Jas said.

"Okay. Go ahead. We'll listen."

"Okay. We are going for a week, Sunday to Sunday... Is that okay with y'all?"

Jas paused for a response.

"Hell yes, honey," Shae said.

"Yeah. That's cool," Los said.

"Okay, good. I was saying we can get a villa! The one I seen had three bedrooms and a living room. Shae, if you are bringing a date, you will have a room, and then the girls will be in the other with me. Los, you will have the third. Is that cool?"

Shae and Los both nodded their heads.

"Okay. We leave in a few weeks, so let's make sure everything is okay on y'all end. My stuff is done and ready to go on mine."

All three agreed and then went their separate ways. Shae sat in the living room thinking about last night with her Mr. Right Now. He was a sight for sore eyes. That man was sexy, light skin, about six feet four, built to perfection like he'd done a jail bid, full beard, and tattoos everywhere. When you thought of him, think of The Game. The way he rocked her world was mind blowing. He fucked her so good that her legs were shaking ten minutes after they finished. They fucked one time before, but Shae knew it wouldn't be more than what it was. She backed off and let him come to her. Shae fell in love too fast, so she kept things to a minimum with these niggas. All men were the same, whether it be a street nigga, businessman, or a damn deacon. They all saw one thing, pussy. She could see herself truly lusting over this man. He was too perfect in her eyes.

Shae sat there reminiscing for a bit about how he'd fucked her in every position in that hotel. They fucked everywhere possible. Shae's body was very sore, but duty called. She decided to get up and go get ready for work. She knew she had some time, so she decided to soak in the bathtub to ease her muscles. She couldn't work with a sore body, and her boo knew that. She knew she couldn't make a career out of her newfound hobby. If the money was as good as it was, she would do it until she couldn't anymore.

She loved fast money. The only thing was that she got addicted to taking Molly. Her best friends would have an all-natural fit if they knew she was doing any drug, especially Carlos. He thought he was someone's damn daddy, always saying what they shouldn't do. Then he hated her job, but like she told him, she did it for the money, the thrill, and the benefits of it.

There was nothing wrong with being a stripper if you asked her. In the words of Ronnie off *Players Club*, "You got to use what you got to get what you want." Shae literally made about $2,000 on a slow night. She was never giving that up. Her mama was a stripper. That was how she met her new sugar daddy. She would worry about her mama if she didn't get a daily text saying she was okay and having a whole ball. Shae was looking for her same come up. She wanted a man to take care of her and give her the world.

Chapter 4

JASMINE

Jas was super happy. She was going to Disney World with her two besties and little sisters. Yas, bish! Yas! Yet and still, all Jas could think was after this Disney World trip, it was time she saved to get her and her little sisters out of there. The projects were no place for them.

Jas went back up to her apartment to go prepare for their trip. She had some last-minute shopping and bills to pay. She kept everything paid a month in advance just for precautions. She was tired of taking care of Lisa, so it was time to move out. Jas walked into her apartment and walked dead into Lisa moaning out to one of her male friends. Jas just shook her head. They looked at her and kept right on fucking. The guy licked his lips and winked at Jas. Jas was tired of it. Jas got dressed for work and proceeded out the door. She got downstairs, and Los was already hugging the block. Their eyes locked, and he just winked at her as the red bone chick walked up to him. Jas kept going. She had a bus to catch. Even though she could've just asked Los, she felt she already took up too much of his time.

Jas went to the bus stop and waited. As she was waiting, a black Audi pulled up in front of her. The cutest white boy ever got out. He was fine, tall, with a dark brown ponytail, but it was shaved on the sides with a design. Icy blue eyes and tattoos were everywhere from the neck down. Now Jas always said she wouldn't date outside of her race, but he could get it.

He walked up to her and said, "What's up, ma. I'm Jason." All Jas could do was shake his hand.

"Hey. I'm Jas."

"It's a pleasure to meet you. Has anyone ever told you that you look like Mya, the singer?" Jas could only nod her head and blush. Jas saw the bus approaching and got up to go to the door. Jason couldn't help but to stare at this beautiful woman before him.

All Jason could say was, "Damn. She fine as fuck!"

Carlos had seen the white boy around a time or two, but he knew he didn't belong on this side of the city. Carlos didn't like anyone to pay Jas any attention. She was pretty. Yeah. He knew that, but in the next few years, she was going to' be his wife. He didn't want another nigga looking at what was his. He knew he had to get his shit together and soon. Jas was a very pretty girl, and any man would be lucky if he got her.

Chapter 5

CARLOS

The red bone sat in front of Los, going off about the way he'd just done her less than a few hours ago. Los was too busy paying attention to Jas and the white boy that was all in her grill. He truly wasn't feeling that bullshit. Los watched him get back in his car and pull from the curb. Jason and Los locked eyes. Jason gave Los a head nod and kept right on about his day. Little did Jason know; Los would kill him over Jasmine. She was off limits to everyone. She was pure, and he wanted her to stay that way. Call him selfish, but only he could have her. Los finally looked at the shawty in front of him and laughed, literally not hearing anything she said the whole time.

"Aye, do you not realize I ain't heard shit you said or even gave you an ounce of attention?"

At this point, Los was highly irritated, mainly with the fact he hadn't acted on his feelings for Jas. He knew once they got to Disney World, he was going to act on his feelings and let her know how he really felt before he lost her altogether. He couldn't take just being her friend any longer, but he had to make sure the timing was right. The red bone looked at him like he had lost his mind.

"Nigga, you weren't just acting like this when we were fucking."

"You ain't my shawty. I don't have to explain shit to you," Los told her before he slid into his car and pulled off. Shawty was going to make the block hot, so it was time to swerve. Twelve stayed looking for any reason to fuck with them block boys.

Los went and grabbed some White Castle before heading over to his boy's house to chill and see when their next re-up would be. When Los got to his boy Dionne's house, he and his baby mama were outside arguing. All Los could think was how glad he was he didn't have those issues.

"Boy, what the hell you got going on?" Los asked his homie.

"Man, she is tripping because she thinks I been with a bitch all night," Dionne replied. Los and Dionne pulled an all-nighter trying to get their last little bit gone before their boss came around. They weren't the big guys, but they were lieutenants in a successful drug ring. They were trying their hardest to climb the food chain. They dealt with their everyday life while still trying to reach their goals.

"Man, come on. Take a ride with me. Y'all both need time to cool down and just talk about it later," Los told Dionne because he knew it was going to' result in Dionne putting his hands on his woman. He didn't want to witness that. He would murk any man for putting their hands on a woman. Los and Dionne got the hell out of there before Dionne's baby mother tried anything else crazy. She was a Jamaican chick, bad as hell but also bat shit crazy. She would throw a damn brick through Los's windshield. Los looked at his boy and knew he was tired and fed up. He could see it all on his face. When his boy was ready to holla at him, he would be all ears. Until then, they rode in silence all the way to the trap.

Los and Dionne ran their trap different from the others. They didn't play the video games and hoes at their trap. You were there to simply get money and make it home. In order to make it home every night, you had to stay ten toes down. Their workers knew if they ever got caught doing bullshit, they were killed on the spot, no questions asked.

Los and Dionne pulled across from the trap and just watched for a bit. Everything was running as smoothly as possible. They got out and went inside the trap. As usual, their boys were working and chilling. Dionne and Los sat at the table. Los knew his boy had a lot on his mind, and he knew this was the time to try and pry. Los had never seen Dionne and his lady argue so much. It was now like an everyday thing.

"Bro, what is going on with you and your baby mother?" Los asked.

"Man, she is tripping for no damn reason. I haven't been fucking with no bitches." Dionne looked like he was in deep thought.

"So, what got her tripping? You got to be giving her some type of fuel, bro."

"Man, just drop it. She just a nagging ass bitch. I ain't trying to hear none of it!" Dionne got up and grabbed a beer and a bottle of Henny out of the fridge.

"Aight, bro. Let's count this money, son." Carlos and Dionne started counting the money for yesterday and what was made so far for today.

Chapter 6

JASMINE

Riding the bus to work was a headache, but it gave Jas time to think and clear her head. She knew she had to plan accordingly for her plans with her sisters and their moves. She just couldn't take living with Lisa any longer. Walking in on her having sex and her partner pretty much undressing her with his eyes made her skin crawl.

Jas had some time before she had to be to work. She checked her bank statement, and she had a little over $12,000. Between Los always putting knots of money in her hand and her paycheck plus tips, it put her in a good space. Jas knew she wouldn't be able to tame a house in downtown Brooklyn on her own, so her next option was to ask her besties to be her roommates. She sent out a group text.

Jas: Guys, do y'all want to be roomies? I was thinking a house in downtown Brooklyn.

Los: What happened? You did not ask this when we were just together.

Shae: Yeah, best. What is wrong?

Jas: I walked in on Lisa getting fucked, and they were dead in the living room. Eww, and the guy winked at me like wtf... I cannot do it no more, y'all. I got to get me and my sisters up out of there. If y'all don't, that is fine. I am gone by July.

Los: Man, I'm down. Why the fuck you aint tell me that when you came downstairs, yo? You just walked to the bus like everything was cool! And who was dude you were talking to at the bus?

Shae: Yeah. I'm down too. Ain't like my mama crackhead ass ever home anyway. I'm sorry you went through that, friend! Wayment... what dude?

Jas: Okay, Los. I'm just fed up and just rather get away from her and them projects. It's okay. And just someone who tried to talk to me, but I just ain't up for it. Shae, okay. That's fine, and thank you, friend. He was fineeeee, but he was no one.

Shae: Okay, so when do we look?

Los: Man, aight, Jas, but I can see what my people got over that way. He got real estate

Shae and Jas both replied "okay".

Jas got off the bus and went to a Starbucks to figure out what all they needed for their new adventure. Once she jotted down some notes and grabbed a caramel latte, she went ahead and took that twenty-minute walk to work. By the time she got there, she had everything figured out and just hoped it went as planned.

Jas's work day went by fast. She grabbed her stuff, heading to the door. As soon as she stepped out, Los was parked, waiting on her. That wasn't a surprise. She walked up to him and gave him a hug while he held the door for her. Los was as real gentlemen to Jas, but these other females he had no respect for. Los got in the car and pulled off.

"How was your day, ma?" Los asked Jas.

"It was okay. Glad I'm off. I'm just ready to go home and get to bed," Jas replied as she stared out the window. Los could tell Jas was stressed out, but he was just waiting on that one call that could turn their life around. He asked Jas if she was hungry. She had food for her sisters but often would forget about herself. Carlos always stopped, and they would grab food and vibe for a bit before going home.

"What you want to eat?" Los asked Jas.

"Hmm… you choose, and I will go off that."

"White Castle okay with you?"

"Yeah. That's fine. Give me a number two with Onion rings and a Sprite!" Jas told Carlos, and he just looked at her and laughed.

"Man, you act like I don't know your order from every restaurant we go to." Jas loved her bond with Los. They were inseparable. In a different world, she could see them in a relationship, married with kids, him off the streets, and her being a businesswoman. That was in a fairytale world. She knew what she wanted in life. Her dream was to be a case worker and to look out for kids. Hopefully she would be able to one day follow her dreams.

Los ordered their food, and they stayed in the parking lot to eat and chop it up.

"So, bestie, whoooo was the girl from earlier? She was pretty and looked angry. What you do to her?"

"Man, you know females are crazy. Why you ain't come ask me to take you to work? You know I hate when you take the bus. It's not safe for you, man."

"I know. I just didn't want to get on your nerves. I know you be hustling."

"Man, Jas, I don't care what I'm doing. When you need to get somewhere, tell me, and I'm taking you. I don't care what I'm doing."

"Okay, Los. I hear you. Dang." Jas and Los finished eating and then headed to the "Bricks". When Los and Jas got to the PJs, he parked his car in the back and walked her to Mrs. Carol's apartment. Once they got to Mrs. Carol's, they fed the girls. While the girls were eating, Jas and Los went to check her apartment to make sure it was safe and clear for the girls. When they got inside, Lisa was laid up with some man, and they were on the couch sleeping naked. Jas hated going through this and couldn't wait to move.

Los walked Jas to grab all of them some overnight bags. Then a thought crossed his mind.

"Jas look at me. Just grab a few bags of clothes for you and the girls. Y'all can stay in my apartment. I don't like worrying about y'all. For real."

"Los, I do not want to put you out of your own home. We will be fine until we find a reasonable house."

"Man, Jas, do what the fuck I said. This ain't up for a debate. Damn." Jas's eyes started to tear up. She already had a lot on her mind, and now Los was yelling at her.

"Jas, I'm sorry for yelling. I just ain't feeling you and your sisters in an unsafe environment."

"Okay, Los." Jas packed two bags for each of them, and Carlos grabbed them from her. Lisa and her company were still in the same spot. When they got to Mrs. Carol's apartment, she grabbed a few things, and they headed to Los's apartment. Los put the girls in Dionne's old room. After he moved, Los put a new bedroom suite in there since he took his. He helped Jas get them situated, and then they went to his room. This wasn't the first time they'd slept in the same bed.

Jas went and showered and then grabbed a T-shirt out of Los's drawer. Los had changed the sheets and blanket by the time she got out of the bathroom. Los and Jas got in the bed and laid side by side. Jas cut off the laptop and rolled over to get some sleep. Los turned toward her and pulled her into him. He whispered into Jas's neck, letting her know he always had them, no matter what. They fell asleep in each other's arms. It felt so right in this moment.

Chapter 7

SHAE

After talking to her two best friends, Shae laid around just thinking how life would be, living with the two very people she grew up with. Anything had to be better than the hell hole she called home in the Bricks. She was ready for the move. She knew she had to work harder now that they all would accumulate bills. Shae was just glad to be sharing a home with her besties. That was the only family she had anyway. Shae decided to get up and get ready for work. While Jas wanted to be a waitress, Shae opted to be a stripper. She tried on many occasions to get Jas to strip because the money was so good, but she understood why Jas wouldn't leave her sister's home alone.

Shae got up and handled her hygiene. Shae decided to just eat at work. She grabbed her car keys and headed to work. Shae got to work fifteen minutes later and walked up to the bar. Shae ordered some wings and fries. While she waited on that, she got a double shot of Henny and headed to the dressing room. She changed into her first outfit for the night. She took a Perc and downed the double shot of Henny as fast as the burn would let her.

When Shae turned around, there was a stripper standing there by the name of Dutchess. Now, Shae couldn't figure why this little skinny bitch was mean mugging her. Shae asked her if she had a damn problem. The girl told her to stay away from her man. She was so confused because she had been with only her new boo who was also the owner of the club where she worked. Shae shook her head and left the dressing room. When Shae got out to the bar to grab her food, all the men were trying to get a lap dance, but she wanted to eat before going on set.

Shae sat and ate her food. She felt a presence behind her. All she could think was *Lord, not again*. She turned around, and her sexy man of a lover was standing there. She couldn't help the lust that filled her eyes. That man was so sexy to her. He leaned into her with his hand sliding between her legs discreetly. He proceeded to tell her to meet him in his office after her set. He liked how wet she got for him. Shae nodded her head and went on to hurry and finish her food.

Shae was the best dancer in the club. From looks to the moves she pulled on the stage; she demanded all the attention when she hit the stage just by the way she moved her body. Shae's cue song to get on stage was Chris Brown's "Another Round". Shae went backstage to take the stage. On cue, her song played. As Shae approached the stage, every eye was on her, strippers included. They looked on with envy as the men looked on in lust. Shae took that stage, twisted her body, and showed how flexible she was. She enjoyed the attention. It made her go even harder. All Shae could see was all the money that was raining down on her. Shae finished off her set and collected her money.

Shae went into the back and headed down the corridor to her lover's office. She knocked twice, and he buzzed her in. His eyes were filled with lust, and he just couldn't help himself. He pulled her in his office and locked the door. He kissed her up against the door and fondled her body. His dick was so hard already from watching her set. He couldn't wait to get inside of her. He pulled her to the couch without breaking their kiss. He laid down, pulling her with him. Shae straddled his lap, feeling his dick wanting to be free. Shae lifted so he could free that sexy dick of his. All eleven inches popped out, and Shae couldn't help but to suck it just the way he liked it. She deep throated him and then pulled it all the way out while still licking the tip. She deep throated again with as much saliva as she could conjure. He couldn't take any more. He had to feel her.

He pulled Shae up and penetrated her. Shae was so tight and wet, and he loved that. Shae being on a perc intensified the feeling of everything. She knew one round wasn't going to be enough for her. He pumped in and out of her, slowly savoring the moment. He felt her nut building and wanted to cum with her because they didn't have a lot of time. The continuous banging on his office door stopped them mid stroke. Mr. Sexy was stuck. He pulled out and fixed his clothes quickly. Shae looked at him while fixing herself, unsure who could be on the other side of the door. When he swung the door open, it was his mistress, Dutchess. What no one knew at the club was that he was married with kids, and that was how he wanted to keep it.

They both looked at Dutchess like she was out of her mind. Shae stood up to leave when Dutchess charged at her. Shae whooped her ass like her mama should have. She was not the one for drama. That was why she didn't have a man now. She was getting ready to walk out, but Devin grabbed her.

"Bae, wait. Where are you going?" Devin asked her.

"I'm getting out of here. I don't do drama. You could have told me you were dealing with that bitch."

"Man, I been stopped fucking with her, ever since the first time we fucked. Man, Shae, I love you." Shae was in shock, but Dutchess was pissed. He'd never told her he loved her.

"Devin, what the fuck? You never told me that, and we been fucking for years." She was his faithful side bitch. He didn't have any feelings for her at all.

"Man, get out before I fire your ass, coming in here on bullshit," Devin told Dutchess. He was tired of her bull.

"Shae, look at me, bae. Did you hear me say I love you? I mean that shit."

"Devin, I love you too, but if it's going to be drama behind us, I don't want it."

"I understand. I got some loose ends to tie up before we go any further."

"That is fine because I'm not ready for a title. I'm focused on securing my future," Shae told Devin. Shae told him she was getting out of there for the night. He kissed her, and she left. Devin needed to know who he was dealing with. She would bust anybody's ass, male or female. She did not play that disrespectful shit.

Chapter 8

CARLOS

Los had been waiting on this one phone call, and it finally came through. Now he was headed to check it out. He pulled up to the two-story six-bedroom, four-bathroom house. His boss man had something in the cut that he was renting for the low, so he jumped on it for them all. This was exactly what they needed, and he just hoped the girls liked it. He planned on furnishing the house before bringing them to see it. Los used majority of the money he hustled for just to make Jas happy. He was not gone stop at nothing to make her happy. Los called his boss man to get his interior decorator to come in and do all the work. Once that was set up and ready, Los headed back to the hood. He knew he would have to hustle day and day out to get his money back up. Los had a little over five hundred thousand put up in his safe. He sent a hundred grand getting this house together.

Couple of days later…

It was now only three days away from their trip, and Los was finishing up last minute dealings with the house. He was getting all his things stored inside. On top of that, he had the kitchen fully stocked. Today was the day all the girls would see the house. Starting with his two best friends, he hit them up in the group chat.

Los: Aye, I need y'all to roll with me for a sec…

Jas: Okay. I'll meet you outside

Shae: Do I have to? I had a long night

Los: Bring your ass on, Shae! NOW…

Shae: Damn. Fine, FATHER. I'm coming…

Jas: LMAO good one, Shae bae

Los sat outside, waiting on the girls. Once they were all in the car, he took them to the house.

"Los, where we are going?" Jas asked, looking around, and Shae just looked on, too tired to even think.

"Just ride and watch!" Los replied. He knew the girls were very impatient, so he turned the radio up. They got to the house, and both girls were deep in thought, not even realizing they were pulling up to a home. Jas finally looked out the window and noticed where they were.

"Los, what is this?" Jas asked him to make Shae turn to look as well. Shae's mouth dropped open at the beauty in front of them.

"Follow me, y'all. This is what we will call home once y'all are ready," Los told the girls. They followed Los into the house. Jas and Shae walked side by side to each room. Once they were finished, Jas ran up to Los and hugged him, saying thank you. Los felt good inside because he could be his best friend's peace.

"When can we move in?" Jas asked, ready to go right now and pack, but Los had other plans for both girls.

"Glad y'all liked it. We can move whenever, but it is better to wait until after our trip," Los said. They all agreed and then left. Their trip was literally two days later. They stopped and got dinner for everyone before going back to the hood where they would only reside for a few more days. Jas was so thankful for Los. He always made shit happen. She would finally be out of the PJs. Her sisters would finally be safe. The PJs consisted of drugs, murders, and prostitution. You could walk out the door and get killed just for being an innocent bystander minding your business. What was so crazy was that was anywhere, but the PJs magnified that chance. Jas refused to let that happen to her sisters. She didn't care what she had to do to get them out of there. He told them to worry about packing after the trip.

Los dropped both the girls back off to the PJs so he could head to the trap to count. When Los got there, his workers were doing their normal. He called Dionne to let him know he was headed there to count. Dionne didn't respond, but lately that was all he ever got from him.

Los started his count in the money counter. Halfway through, his phone went off. It was his plug. He always called when it was close to time to re-up. They talked for a little. Los told him he was almost at the mark. They disconnected so Los could continue his count. The way he ran his operation was that they had three safes. In two of them, the lieutenant had the code in order to put the money from their earnings in there. He was the only one besides Los and Dionne who had the code. The floor safe, no one knew about but Dionne and Los. Their operation was fairly thought out and planned to keep them all safe. Los didn't even keep the same trap running. Each area had three traps that they alternated throughout the year in case the feds or some jack boys wanted to try some bullshit. Los finished his count and then placed the money in the floor safe. His re-up was the day after he got back from the trip with the girls.

Chapter 9

JASMINE

It was the day they left for Disney World, and Jas was so excited. She had never been out of NYC. Everyone was nervous about flying. The girls still didn't know where they were going. They were just was ready to go. It was four o'clock in the morning, and the girls were grabbing their stuff to head to Los's car so that they could make it for their 6:00 a.m. flight. Jas double checked everything the night before, so they were ready to go. They all climbed in the elevator.

Once downstairs, Los grabbed their bags and put them in the trunk. The girls were already buckled in. As Jas was getting in, Shae walked up to Los's car and passed him her bag. They all headed to the airport. Once there, they went through security check and took a seat until they were boarding. Shae and Jas headed to get everyone breakfast until the flight was over. Everyone was nervous but excited as well. Shae kept going live on Facebook and Instagram. She was ready for her boo to arrive the next day. He had last minute touches to handle before he left.

After an hour, it was time to board their flight. They flew for a few hours. Once they landed and got a rental car, they were headed to their destination. Jas was so excited to see her babies' faces. She went live once they got close. When the girls saw Disney World, their faces made Jas tear up. The happiness was all she wanted, and that was all she would ever give them. She was ready to explore the park with her sisters and take a lot of pictures. She wanted them to remember this forever. This was their first time out of NYC, and it was beautiful here. Jas was just as mesmerized as the girls. She was going to make sure the girls got everything they asked for.

The weather was so hot. They were all tired and ready to get to the hotel. Jas booked them at the palace. It was a hotel on Disney World property. They would be dead in the middle of the park. It looked like a princess castle. All the things they had in the park and hotel was bound to make their week extra fun. Jas couldn't wait, but for now she just wanted to get them settled in. She needed a nap.

CHAPTER 10

Carlos

They all checked into their room and were jet lagged. Shae retired to her room, and the girls went to theirs. Jas wasn't tired, so she just went ahead and sat in the living room. Los placed his bag in his room and decided to join Jas on the couch. He grabbed a bottle out of the mini bar and rolled him some weed. He needed it right now. Jas looked at him and could tell something was bothering him. They took some shots back to back just to unwind. Jas could feel the tingle in her body from the alcohol, but she knew what her mind, body, and heart were telling her. Los had always been there for her and made a way when he didn't have to. That made her love him even more after the house.

Los looked at Jas and couldn't help himself. He leaned over and kissed her. To his surprise, she didn't object or pull away. The kiss deepened. Los stopped himself and looked at Jas. He asked if she was sure, and she said yes. Los picked her up and carried her to his room. He closed the door with his foot and laid her on the bed. They kissed so passionately. Los took his time with Jas. He stripped her down and then himself. Los trailed kisses down to her pearl and licked, sucked, and nibbled on it. Jas was so wet. This was her first time, and the sensation was out of this world. As her stomach tightened up, she tried to push his head away, but he wasn't letting up. Jas told him she had to pee, and that made him go even harder. Once Jas came in his mouth, he was very satisfied. Los knew he had to take his time with Jas.

He eased onto the bed and laid between her legs. Jas was out of breath just looking at him. He loved the way she looked at him in admiration. Los asked Jas if she was ready. He told her once he went in that she was his forever. Jas just nodded. Los placed his dick at her center and pushed in a little. Jas tensed up from the pain. Los told her to relax. He asked if she trusted him. She told him yes. He kissed her passionately and pushed in more. Los was working with ten inches and quite thick. He finally got in and had to stop and enjoy the tightness and wetness of her pussy. Jas moaned in Los's ear, and it drove him crazy. They were falling deeper for each other.

Los fucked Jas for two hours straight. The only issue was that he never pulled out. He came in Jas twice. Jas and Los were so tired. They just pulled the cover up and dozed off together. Los knew this was the start of their newfound relationship, and he was ready. He didn't think he would ever get this chance with Jas. He swore that he was going to do right by her by any means, and Los meant every word.

The next day…

Los woke up and looked next to him. He was glad to finally get the woman he had been craving. He leaned over and kissed Jas all over her face. Jas stirred in her sleep. Los took it one step further. He trailed kisses down to her pearl. By this time, Jas was up and loving the feeling. Los just wanted to please her and take all her worries and stress away. Jas gripped his head with her thighs. That made Los go even harder. He felt Jas's leg clench and shake. She was at her peak. He took his index finger and middle finger and made a come here gesture in her honey pot. They knew if they didn't stop right then, they wouldn't make it out that room. Los pulled away, pecked Jas once more, and told her come on. They had a busy day ahead.

Jas got up to handle her hygiene. Los admired the woman she was. He'd seen the little redbone calling his phone back to back, so he put her on the block list. It was time to block all his old hoes. He wasn't taking any chance of losing the one woman God had created so perfect for him. Jas was his soulmate. He could tell from the feelings he got when he was around her. Since she had been in his bed every night, Los made sure he was home to lay next to her and eat dinner with them. He loved having them in his personal space. It gave him more of a reason to go hard. He now had a reason to live, a reason to hustle.

Jas came out of the bathroom and started to get dressed, but Los had other plans. He wanted to feel her tightness before they got their day started. Los started kissing on Jas's neck. He pushed her slowly onto the bed. Los entered her slowly. Jas was still extra tight, and he loved the feeling. Los pushed in her inch by inch. Jas was easing up. Los was packing. With Jas, he made love to her. Once Los was all the way in, he deep stroked her. Jas was trying to moan as low as possible, but that wasn't working, so Los kissed her while he brought her to her peak back to back. Los was moaning like a bitch, and that was not like him. He couldn't help it. He had to bring Jas to one more nut before he came. He sped up his strokes. When he felt Jas's pussy contract, he knew she was near. Jas's legs started shaking, and then he felt her nutting. Los let go of his nut while Jas rode the wave of her orgasm. Los looked down at her and kissed her on the nose. He was deeply in love with this woman and couldn't get enough. They got in the shower together and had sex once more before they got ready.

CHAPTER *11*

Shae

Shae got up to go make breakfast for everyone, but a wave of nausea hit her out of nowhere. She chucked it up to the flight from before. She sent a text over to Devin, a.k.a. Mr. Sexy.

Shae: Hey, babe. What time you landing?

Devin: I just landed. I'll text you when I am settled. I brought my sister and her kids as well. Hope you don't mind. They needed the vacation.

Shae: That's fine, babe. I cannot wait to see you

Devin: I cannot wait to see you either, babe. I love you

Shae: Aww, babe. I love you too

Shae was speechless. Every time Devin told her he loved her, it was a shock, but she could not lie about her feelings. She was feeling something. She told Devin she wasn't ready for a relationship, but with him, she was ready to try. She loved him just as much as he loved her. She just let her fear keep her from taking that leap of faith.

She got up to handle her hygiene before heading to the kitchen. She realized they had yet to go to the store, so instead she called room service for a breakfast spread of pancakes, waffles, turkey bacon, scrambled eggs with and without cheese, oatmeal, grits, fruits, orange juice, and apple juice. Then she returned to her room where she prepared for the day. She heard the knock and went to get the door. It was Devin. She gave him a quick hug and kiss. Right when she reentered the room, there was another knock. Devin got a little scared because little did Shae know; it was his wife and children with him. He had his wife thinking they were on vacation and a business trip. He looked at the door and breathed a sigh of relief when he saw room service entering. Shae grabbed the cart and tipped the waiter. She began putting the spread on the table. She then proceeded to wake everyone up for breakfast. She and Devin then sat at the table waiting. What shocked her the most was seeing Jas and Los all lovey dovey, coming out the room. They both stopped and looked at Shae. She was glad they did finally follow their feelings since she now had her own man.

Jas and Los sat down. When Los looked up and saw his boss man, they both were just as shocked. Los asked Devin what the hell he was doing there. He told Los he was there on business and to chill with his lady. Now Los knew that was some bullshit. This was a married man. He knew he couldn't intervene, because that was his money. The girls then came out. They said grace and all ate while planning what all they wanted to do that day. The women cleaned up while the fellas sat on the couch and watched sports highlights. Los whispered to Devin.

"What you doing here? Where is the missus and kids?"

"They are up in the penthouse. Look, young blood. I got this. Don't worry. Shawty is in good hands. I may be with my wife, but I don't love her at all."

"Aight, man. I'll back off."

About thirty minutes later, everyone was ready to go. They all headed to the park for a day of fun. They all went from ride to ride. Today they were getting on roller coasters. Jas stayed down because she was afraid of heights. She didn't play that getting on shit that could get stuck in midair. Hell no. Call her scary or whatever. She didn't give a damn. She wasn't getting on it. Now when they played the games or rode the train and boat, she was all for it. Tomorrow they would explore the first water park. There was so much for them to do, and Jas was too ready. They took picture after picture and couldn't wait to upload it. They did this for hours until they were all hungry and tired. They grabbed some pizza and headed back to their room.

Jas and Los went to one room. The girls went to their room. Devin and Shae went to hers. Devin locked the door behind them. He walked up on Shae and slid his hand up under her dress, playing with her swollen pearl. He inserted two fingers to see how wet she was. She looked deep into his eyes and wrapped her arm around his neck. Her legs were starting to get weak as the orgasm was building. He started to feel her cum seeping into his hand. Her knees buckled, and he caught her. He walked her back to the bed where he laid her down and climbed on top of her. His goal was to fuck her to sleep and go to his room tonight. He made love to her for two hours, watching the love faces she made. He loved seeing those faces on her. It made him even harder.

Devin came in Shae after her tenth nut, and he was satisfied. Shae was out like a light. Devin kissed her forehead, put some money on the table, and left. Shae jumped up in the middle of the night to throw up again. By this time, she knew something was terribly wrong. She decided to just wait until they got home and settled before taking the test. She just hoped Devin didn't notice. She saw the money on the table and shrugged it off to him going to check on his sister and her kids. She got back in bed and laid down.

CHAPTER 12

Devin

When Devin got back to his room, it was a little after 3:00 a.m. His wife was wide awake and fuming. When she heard the door open, she just looked at her husband. Devin thought he would be able to sneak in and shower before going to bed next to his wife. She walked up to Devin and smelled another woman all over him. She smacked Devin so hard that his reflexes made him smack her ass back. Devin was tired of his wife putting her hands on him. He hated hitting her. That wasn't the life he wanted his kids accustomed to. Devin walked away and went to shower before bed. He was tired of trying to hold on to his marriage for his kids. His wife wasn't the least bit innocent. How did you cheat in a city that your husband ran? He was just fed up, so once he got back to the city, he was filing for divorce. He knew she wasn't going to go down without a fight, so he had to play his cards right. His wife knew way too much.

The next morning...

Devin slept on the couch, so his body wasn't agreeing with him one bit. He grabbed his packed bags and carried them out the door. He took the elevator to Shae's floor and exited. He knocked on the door. Because her room was right by the door, he knew she would answer. Shae came to the door half sleep. She figured it was him, so she opened the door and went back to bed. He brought all his bags in and locked up. He climbed in bed with Shae. This was his first time laying up with Shae, and he had to admit it felt damn good. He wrapped his arm around her and pulled her close. He found comfort with Shae. A few hours later, Shae and Devin were woken up to his phone going off continuously. He instantly thought something was wrong. He looked to see that it was his wife. He ignored the call and immediately blocked her calls. He then sent her a text asking if everything was okay. He then put his phone on silent. Shae looked at him and got up to go handle her hygiene.

Devin walked in the bathroom to explain that it was business, and this time was all about them. She couldn't understand why he was explaining. They were not in a relationship, so there was no need to. They showered together and met everyone in the living room. Everyone went out for brunch and went to explore the water park. They stayed out there for about four hours and decided to go back to the room to just spend the day watching movies together and eating. Devin missed these kinds of times with his wife and kids, but it was hard to do when she was always bitching.

Devin cuddled up to Shae and dozed off. Devin got up because he was hungry. Shae was still sleep, but Devin wanted to get dinner for them. The park had some romantic attractions that they could go to. He woke her up to get dressed for their night out. He didn't want her to get all fancy... just some laid back attire. They both were in a jogging suit. When they got out, Los and Jas were chilling on the couch. Devin told them they should join. Shae begged Jas to go. Her middle sister was old enough to babysit. She told them where they were going and set some rules. The girls felt Jas deserved some *her* time, so they promised to sit tight.

The two couples left out for dinner first. They ate dinner and drank. From there, they tried the tunnel of love. It was a little dove raft, and it was a four-seater. They were on the ride for fifteen minutes. It was so beautiful to the girls. Los and Jas took some pics while on the ride. Everyone was feeling themselves and ready to get back to the room. They took the long way just to enjoy the nighttime scene. Both couples took a few pictures together and then a group pic. Los was ready to get back, so they headed to the room.

When they got there, Jas and Los showered together and headed into bed to cuddle and watch movies. Jas uploaded all her pictures to her Instagram and Facebook. She tagged Los and Shae in their pictures. She then put her phone on "do not disturb" to enjoy her time with her man. Jas was one step closer to happiness. They dozed off. Tomorrow they would be going through the France and Africa part of the park, and Jas was ready.

CHAPTER 13

Jasmine

They explored every aspect of the park. There were over fifty attractions. The girls loved every bit of the park. They only had one more day left at the park. On the very last day, Jas got a call from Mrs. Carol. She picked up all happy because her and Los had been having a good time. She knew once they got back that they were going to be busy.

"Hey, Mrs. Carol. How are you? You miss us yet?"

Mrs. Carol was like their grandmother, so Jas didn't think anything about the call until Mrs. Carol spoke.

"Hey, love. How is y'all trip going? When will y'all be returning?"

Jas could sense the hesitation in Mrs. Carol's voice. She didn't know what could be wrong.

"Mrs. Carol, what is wrong? You okay? We come back tomorrow night. Do u need me to come back now?"

Jas was in a panic and tensed up. Her voice made Carlos sit up in the bed and ask her what was wrong, but Jas ignored his worried eyes, waiting on an answer from Mrs. Carol.

"Honey, I'm sorry to tell you this while you are on vacation, but your mother was shot three times. She died on the scene. I'm sorry, honey. You know you girls are like family. I'm here if y'all ever need me. I love y'all."

"We love you too, Mrs. Carol. We will see you tomorrow as soon as we get back." Jas hung up the phone and was looking in space. Los asked what was wrong, and Jas let out a gut-wrenching cry. Carlos grabbed hold of her and kept asking what was wrong. By the time she was done explaining, everyone was walking into their room. Jas couldn't even look at her sisters, because she knew she would have to be the one to break the news to them. Carlos told everyone to give them a minute while they talked. Everyone walked out the room.

"Bae, if you don't know nothing else, just know I got y'all. Man, I've loved you my whole life, and I'll die to make sure y'all will always be good. Do you hear me? Y'all are my life, and I'll do anything for y'all."

"Thank you, bae. I too have been in love with you. What am I going to tell the girls though? I do know one thing. I want Mrs. Carol with us."

"Aight, bae. That's fine. We will talk to her when we get back. After we tell everyone, we are going to book new flights. I love you."

"Okay. I love you too." Los and Jas got up to go tell everyone the bad news. They met with everyone in the living room. Jas sat on the couch and told both the girls to come sit. She explained to them that their mother was killed and that they would have to prepare for the funeral. She explained to them that they would have to take the next flight home to start packing.

Los and Jas went back to the room where she booked six tickets for the flight. She laid down while Los got their things packed. He wanted her to get as much rest as possible, before getting to NYC. She had a long stressful week coming, and he wanted his baby to be able to get through it. He was going to be by her side through it all. Little did they all know, hell was brewing.

Their flight was scheduled to leave in seven hours. They would be on the six o'clock flight. Los laid down to catch a nap. He knew he would have to catch up with his team as soon as he got back so that they could get back to work. He also had to talk to his boss man before they took flight.

Jas laid with Los. Her mind was all over the place. Even though Lisa was her mother, she didn't have the money to move and bury Lisa. She had a big decision to make. What was more important? Giving her sisters a better life or burying Lisa. She knew Lisa used to work. She wasn't sure if Lisa had insurance or anything that would help. Lisa used to tell her when she died, she wanted her ashes spread over the ocean so that she could be extra free. Jas made a note to herself that she would have her cremated, and then about a month later, she would have her ashes spread.

Once landed...

Los, Jas, and the girls climbed into his car while Devin and Shae climbed into hers. She was not going to let her best friend go through this alone. They all went to the new house. Once at the house, everyone went to their rooms and unpacked. Instead of Jas going into her own room, she took her stuff to Carlos's room. Everyone was surprised that all their belongings were now in this house.

Carlos stayed downstairs with Devin while the ladies put the things away. Once all their belongings were put up, they all piled into Los's Escalade truck and headed over to Mrs. Carol's building. When they all got to Mrs. Carol's building, they could see the crime scene from where Lisa was killed. They made it to Mrs. Carol's floor and knocked on her door. Mrs. Carol came to the door and let everyone in. She looked so worn out and tired, like the weight of the world was on her shoulders. All four girls ran up to Mrs. Carol. She hugged them all. Jas pulled away first and told Mrs. Carol she wanted her and the kids to move with them. They had the room. She looked at everyone and broke down.

Mrs. Carol grew up in the projects, so this move was something new for her. She also knew she couldn't leave Jas to raise the girls on her own, so she agreed. Los told her to leave everything. The movers would get it. She grabbed the kids and her purse. They all proceeded out. Los knew every apartment had roaches, no matter how clean a motherfucker was. He had all three of their apartments bombed and fumigated. Hers was no different. He didn't want any of those gang banging roaches Crip walking across their counters at the new house.

They all left and headed to their new residence, hoping that was the last of their sorrows for a long while. When they got to the house, they all went inside. They removed their shoes and coats. Jas showed Mrs. Carol around. While she was doing that, Carlos was shaking Mrs. Carol's house coat. Devin was too amused. He looked at Carlos like a little brother. These past few days showed him a new him. It was time he taught Los the connect part of the streets. He wanted to ease Carlos into the newfound leadership. He knew with the drama with his wife, anything could happen, so he had to be ten steps ahead of her. A woman scorned could be a man's biggest downfall. He tried to keep as much of his street life away from her as possible, but she still knew too much. Last thing he needed was the police looking into his club and restaurant. Devin knew it was time to cut back from the streets. He would teach Carlos the ropes and then just get his cut.

CHAPTER 14

Los

Los went to check on the ladies before he went with Devin. Jas had been trying to be strong for her sisters, but because of their pain, she was hurting for them. Shit was crazy for him. He needed a strong ass drink, a blunt, and some pussy from his wifey. After checking with the girls, he headed to wherever Devin wanted to go. Devin was ready to step down. He knew Carlos had the potential to be the boss. Devin took Los by the different traps, letting him see how they were running on the other side. Devin took him to the west, the south, and the north. Those were all ran by different head niggas. Carlos ran the east, so that would be the last one. Carlos looked at the way those niggas ran their traps and saw a lot of loop holes and problems. On the way to the last set before they hit his traps, Devin asked what he thought about those few.

"Los, what's up? Why you are looking like that?"

"Can I be honest as fuck? I'm just looking at it as keeping us all free."

"Go ahead. I'm listening."

"Man, first off, I see a few things with them traps that's bound to get us knocked. Look at how it looks. Look at the traffic. That shit screams trap house. Then the workers too busy bullshitting to even pay attention. They got product everywhere, doors unlocked, and niggas playing the game."

"I'll take that into consideration. We will talk."

"Aight." After they left the last set, Carlos headed to his traps. He didn't tell his team he was back just yet. He wanted to see how they were acting. They pulled up to the trap about thirty minutes later. They got out at the trap and walked right in. Los walked in and just watched. He couldn't believe what the fuck was going on. All he could think was where the fuck was Dionne. These niggas were having an all-out party in the trap. Devin stepped back to see how Los would handle himself. Los sent Dionne a text saying 911. Los removed his gun and shot in the air. Everyone froze in place and looked at him. His team looked like they'd seen a ghost.

"Everyone get the fuck out nowwwww! You niggas in the fucking living room right now," he practically growled at his workers. He didn't get a response from Dionne, and that pissed him off even more.

"What the fuck are y'all thinking? Who fucking idea was this? Have y'all seen Dionne? While y'all partying, where all my shit?"

One dude looked around and just decided to answer.

"Man, we been getting it all week. We just wanted to unwind. Dionne upstairs. He got too lifted. He let us throw the party. Everything is in the safe." Los went upstairs to see where Dionne was. Dionne was passed out on the bed. Los shook him awake.

"Aye, bruh. Get up! What the fuck is you doing, bruh? Is you trying to get us fucking knocked!" Los yelled at Dionne.

"Nigga, you not my motherfucking boss. Nigga, you been on vacation while I stayed here and made shit move. Fuck you, nigga!" Dionne jumped up and yelled. Los was very confused. He didn't know his best friend felt this way. Devin stepped in.

"He isn't your boss, but I am. He is the boss in training. I don't like the way my trap is being ran. Get it cleaned up. This your first and final warning." Devin walked out. Los was even more confused, but he ain't have no complaints. Dionne just stayed there spaced out, so Los walked downstairs to his workers and told them to get it cleaned up. He left out the door and got in the car with Devin.

They decided to head to his strip club next. Los wanted to ask about what he'd said, but right now wasn't the time. When they got there, there was a section already ready with two bottles of Ace of Spades. They sat down and rolled up a few blunts. This was well needed for both men. They were kicking back and enjoying the show when the red bone he'd fucked walked in their section. He didn't know she was a stripper. She sat next to him. He glanced over, not trying to give her any ideas.

"I've been calling you. I really need to talk to u," shawty said to him. He told her he was good and kept smoking. Shawty got mad and told him, "I'm pregnant, and I'm keeping it. I'll be in fucking touch!"

She walked off. Los couldn't believe what she'd just said. He knew it was time to go home and tell his old lady. He and Devin left the strip club. His mood was all messed up. Right when he got the girl he'd been dreaming for, some bullshit happened. When they arrived at the house, all the lights were off except the living room. He and Devin entered the home. Jas and Shae were sitting on the couch, eating snacks and watching Netflix. Los walked up on Jas and kissed her. She embraced his kiss. He sat next to her and sighed. She looked at him and could see all the worry on his face.

"Baby, what's wrong?" Jas asked him.

"Man, bae, I got some shit to talk to you about! Can we go to the room?" Los asked her. Jas and Los retired to the room. They sat on the bed where Jas laid down. Los laid his head on her chest, and she rubbed his head.

"Jas, the red chick you seen me talking to in the PJs… she pregnant. I don't know if it's mine. Then she said she is keeping it! Bae, I don't know the bitch name. Ugh! How the fuck I slip like that, man? Jas, I'm sorry. For real." Carlos poured his heart out to Jas.

"Bae, at the time it happened, we were friends. I can't be mad. What I will say is I'm not going for the baby mama drama. In time we will tell, but for now, we just got to deal with it, Los. Thank you. You have been there for me and my sisters, and I love you for that."

"Always, bae. I love you too." She bent down and kissed him. They cuddled and went to bed, both with so much on their minds. Was Jas ready to deal with a baby mother while she was so young? Jas had loved Los for a long time, so she was just going to go with the flow for now.

CHAPTER 15

Shae

Devin came and sat next to Shae. He pulled her into his lap. This was his moment of truth. He no longer wanted to lie to Shae. He felt some shit brewing nearby. He needed peace somewhere.

"Bae just listen to what I'm about to say, and let me explain before you jump to conclusions," Devin told Shae, and she nodded, ready for him to tell her it was over and that he wanted someone else. She was very tense.

"Okay. Here it goes. I have a wife and kids, but Shae, I don't love her. I love you. The only reason I'm still with her is because of everything she knows about me and my lifestyle. I see that look. I'm more than the owner of the strip club and restaurant. I'm the connect for New York. I supply all five boroughs. I'm just trying to get out before I divorce her. Bae, I have never felt this way about no chick. I'm in love with you, and I'll make sure you and my baby are straight… Don't look like that. I can tell u pregnant. That pussy be super wet and gushy. I'll have to keep your sexy ass pregnant, but for now we going to do what we need to in order to secure our future. Aight?"

Shae was very speechless. The pregnancy part and marriage part were mind blowing. She was just ready to lie down with her man and figure everything out tomorrow. Shae and Devin headed to bed. The next day, everyone was up and moving. The kids were staying in the house with Mrs. Carol. Jas was headed to work an early shift. Shae was headed to enroll in college. Devin wanted her to get a business degree. She was not about to be a stripper and carry his child.

Shae went to NYU to sign up. Devin gave her a blank check for tuition cost and books. She signed up for class and went to the bookstore to get her books and laptop. She did most of her classes online. She left campus and made an emergency visit to her doctor. Shae filled out all her necessary paperwork and waited to be called to the back. Shae was called back less than ten minutes later. They took her weight and blood pressure. They then asked for a pee sample. They gave her a gown and sat her in a room. A few minutes later, the doctor came in the room.

"Hey, Shae. I've got good news. Congratulations, Mommy to be."

"Oh, wow… I mean I had a feeling, but wow. I mean shit… I mean uh… just let me shut up. I'm sorry." Shae was so worked up. She was rambling.

"Okay, Mommy. Do you want to see baby?" Shae nodded her head. Once all measurements were taken and the heartbeat was heard, Shae walked out, scheduling her next appointment and getting her vitamins. She sent Devin a text confirming his suspicions. She was indeed four and a half months pregnant. How could she let that slip by her? She'd gotten pregnant the very first time they'd fucked in his office. After that, she avoided him until one night he cornered her in the dressing room. That was the beginning of their love affair. Now it was them against the world. She was going to make sure her man was 100 percent. She was starting to love him. He was her man now, and she wasn't letting him go. His wife just didn't know what she was up against. Shae would kill her if she had to and raise her kids like they were hers. They had a child to build for now, so Shae knew it was time to get her shit together and soon. She texted Jas and told her she was going to be an auntie and god mommy. She wanted to celebrate something good happening after everything that had been going on. She told Jas and Devin both about dinner and made reservations for the family to go out.

CHAPTER *16*

Los

Los and Devin were headed back to the main trap where they had a meeting with each crew. Things were getting ready to change. Los already knew everything about the game except the connect. It was now time for the transition. Los would no longer be just a lieutenant. Los was taking Devin place so that he can step down. Devin knew if anyone would be good at it, it would be Los. He was hungry for it. He paid attention to detail and left no room for mistakes. He was determined to grind and make a way for his little family. Nothing was gone get in the way of Los money.

They sat down with each crew and broke down every detail. Los was switching traps, lieutenants, street soldiers, and he was adding traps and drugs. He wanted it all, and he was going to get it. He wasn't willing to do it the sloppy way either. He had to truly think smart. He had a baby on the way. He finally had asked Devin what old girl's name was. It was Jacinda. He just hoped she stayed out the way and didn't give him hell. He knew how Jas and Shae could get. They finished up with the meeting, letting everyone know they were going to start with the east side. They new go to person would be Los.

Los went to the one place he knew Dionne was going to be, the trap on the south. He let everyone know about the meeting, and Dionne didn't show. They pulled up and went in. They had all traps shut down while they were making changes. Los just had a funny feeling. When he walked in, Dionne wasn't there. He called Dionne back to back with no answer. He went to all three safes, even the one the crew didn't know about. When he saw all the safes empty, he knew the one nigga he trusted had shited him.

Carlos walked to the living and told Devin to come on. In the car, he explained that Dionne hit them and hard. Devin loaded up his gun. He asked Carlos if he was strapped. Los told him he was, and they proceeded to Dionne's baby mama's house. When they got there, everything was gone. There was a for rent sign and all. Carlos knew this would put a damper in his plans for him and his family. Los knew he was going to find Dionne and kill him. He now knew there were no friends in this game. Devin knew it was time to beef up security on all the ladies. He knew to add security to follow them as well. They didn't know who Dionne had working with him for him to be that brave. They knew he was on borrowed time. He'd better be gone from New York altogether. They made the command to have security set up for the girls and their homes. Los sent Jas a text, telling her stay put. He needed to talk to her.

Now it all went by who to trust in a situation like this. The guys searched high and low looking for Dionne but couldn't locate him. Devin decided to finally call in reinforcements. He called his plug. His plug, James, was in Cuba and could track anybody down. He knew when it came to James's money, he played no games. Devin dialed James up.

"Devin, now what do I owe this pleasure?"

"Mannnnn, we got an issue on our hands! A lot of our girls and her friends went missing by an angry worker," Devin told James in code.

"Send me his phone number, name, and a possible pic. I'll have my guys on it. Oh yeah, Devin. We will meet soon!"

"I know. Thanks for the help." He looked over to Los and asked for Dionne's info. While Los ran it off to him, he sent it over to James.

When he got to the house, the girls were sitting in the living room with Miss Carol. He didn't want to scare the girls, so he just told them that they had a situation and always needed the girls to keep security for everyone's safety. He told them to make sure they texted them and let them know when they would be leaving the house and where they would be. The girls didn't like that idea at all, but they knew what Carlos did for a living, so it was better to be safe than sorry. Los knew with power came more money and more enemies. It was time to secure his family. He seen all the potential in his traps and he planned on making it triple. Los Took traps that was only making $25,000 and turned them into traps that now made $1 million in a month. Traps that was making $100,000 was now making 2 million in a month. It was not a drug that they didn't serve. Los had a family he needed to feed and he refused to not feeding them.

Two months later..

CHAPTER 17

Devin

James hit Devin back with info on Dionne. After waiting a few months for the info they finally got him. He was trying to lay low in Brooklyn. His cousin that he was staying with couldn't keep his mouth shut. He was bragging on the lick they'd hit. They had to hurry and get their shit back before someone ran up in there. After they all finished eating, the guys headed out to handle this business. Devin informed Los of everything about Dionne. He couldn't believe it, so they headed to scope out the address. When they got there, they saw Dionne and his baby mama standing on the porch talking. For once, they were getting along. They sat scoping out the place for several hours after Dionne's baby mama left.

Los and Devin knew it was well over time to make their move. They put the silencers on the guns and went through a back alley. They came up to a back window where they saw a TV on. Devin was good at picking locks, so they went to the back door. They gained entry and moved as quietly as they could. With this being an old house, they were making sure they didn't hit any weak boards that would squeak. Upstairs, it sounded like someone was getting fucked. They were loud as shit. Crazy part about it was they didn't remember seeing any females come in. They knew there were three niggas in there.

They walked to the bedroom on the right and peeked in. They saw a body. They walked over to the bed to see who it was. They didn't know him. Devin grabbed a pillow from the bed, put it over the man's head, and pulled the trigger twice. They wore gloves just for that reason. They crept upstairs. There were three doors. They tried both on the right just to make sure they both were empty. When they got to the room on the left, they saw Dionne bent over getting fucked by the other nigga, moaning like a bitch. They were so caught up that they didn't even know they were being watched. He told Dionne to turn over and catch this nut. When Dionne did, his face went pale. The nigga was jacking his dick, so he didn't realize there were niggas in the room.

He told Dionne, "Come on, nigga. Don't worry about your cousin. I be fucking him too." Dionne looked at the nigga like *what the fuck*. Los had heard enough. He shot the nigga in the head. He went down like a ton of bricks. Dionne was shocked. He'd never seen this side of Los. That was why he felt he could rob him, but now he knew he'd fucked up. Devin went to one side, and Los went to the other. Devin let Los do the talking. He knew he had to get some shit off his chest. He just listened.

"Nigga, where is my shit? And before you lie about it, your dead ass, gay ass cousin been running around bragging about the lick y'all hit, so spill it, my nigga." Los was beyond hurt. This was his brother at one point.

"Man, it's in the safe. Come on. Don't kill me. I got kids that need me. The combo is twenty-seven, eight, nineteen." Los couldn't do shit but laugh. Did this nigga just say no to kill him?

"Nigga, did you say don't kill you? You got to be joking. Do you know the opportunity you passed up? You were going to be right beside me, nigga. My equal. I talked Devin into splitting that shit down the fucking middle just so your snake ass could eat like me. See you in hell, motherfucker." Los blew his brains out and went to the safe. There was less drugs but way more money in there, so he wasn't complaining. They got the hell out of dodge. Devin sent a text to the cleanup crew, and they left. He called James on the burner phone and told him it was done. He told Devin he would be in the states in two days and to be ready. Devin knew it was time for James and Carlos to meet. He didn't know the drama that would stir up from this meeting. It took years for los to reach boss status but now that he was finally there you couldn't tell los nothing. Devin gave los all the rest of the work he had. It was now all in Los hands. He knew he was going to have to go in with Los on this house they wanted for the girls. He stopped by his strip club to grab the cash for there soon to be new homes.

CHAPTER 18

Jas

Jas had been really fatigued and sick lately, but she couldn't figure out why. It had been a few weeks since they'd been back from Disney World, and it didn't seem like things were getting any better. She didn't have a funeral for her mom, because she didn't have any family, so she just had her cremated.

Jas went to Walgreens to get a pregnancy test. She wanted to take it when no one was around. When she got back to the house, she went ahead and took the test. It came back positive. Jas was so scared. She was only eighteen and already raising her two sisters. What the fuck was she going to do with a baby? Where was she allowed to get an abortion? She kept thinking maybe she could sneak and do it, but she also knew Carlos wouldn't go for it. She knew everyone would be so excited about her being pregnant.

Jas could not understand how they were so careless Jas went and laid on the bed. She cried herself to sleep not realizing she left the test on the sink. Los woke Jas up kissing all over her face down, then down her neck. He kissed all the way down to her Pearl, but Jas really wasn't in the mood. Jas told Carlos they needed to talk but he wasn't listening. Jas was scared out of her mind about being pregnant. Jas pushed Carlos off her and told him they need to talk. Carlos got irritated with Jas all he wanted to do was make love to his woman and get some sleep. Los had to be prepared to hit the streets. Los and Devin were still waiting on an answer from the plug. When Los went into the bathroom, he seen the pregnancy test sitting on the sink. Carlos stared at the pregnancy test that is in his hand. He couldn't believe Jas was pregnant. He knew they haven't been using protection, but he thought his pull-out game was a little bit stronger. The only thing that went through Los mind was, *what was he going to do with two newborns!* Los went back into the room to talk to Jas about her pregnancy.

"Damn, babe. You pregnant?" Carlos asked Jas.

"Yes. I'm guessing so. I want to make a doctor's appointment just to be sure. What are we going to do?" Jas asked.

"What the fuck you mean what we going to do? What you think we going to do? We're going to raise a damn child. Fuck you looking like that for?"

"Carlos don't be fuckin' cussing at me. I asked the damn question. You already got a possible child on the way. What are we going to do with two?" Jas asked out of frustration.

"Man, come here, cry baby. Look at you! Damn. My baby having my baby." Carlos kissed Jas passionately and continued what he'd started. They fucked for two hours straight, not leaving any body part untouched. He knew he was in love with Jas, and that was all that mattered. She was his peace away from the streets. He felt it was time for him to make better choices for his family. After the long talk he had with Devin, he had the realtors looking for a new house that was bigger and more secure. Now that he had two babies on the way, he knew he had no choice but to expand.

Carlos laid down and watched Jas sleep. She was so beautiful to him. He couldn't wait to see her big and pregnant. He promised to so right by Jas. She scheduled her appointment for tomorrow, so they would find out how far she was. Jacinda told him she had one the following day. This was about to be a headache. He knew she was going to be the baby mama from hell. She called all day pretty much for nothing. He planned to sit down and talk with her to let her know she couldn't keep doing that. Once she got about four months, he was going to do a DNA test. He wanted to be sure before he invested his time in her baby. Carlos wound up dozing off, holding Jas with his hand on her stomach.

They got through Jas's appointment. She was six weeks pregnant. She was scheduled for another appointment in a month. Carlos got the call he was waiting on. The realtor called for him to come see the new house. It was a forty-five-minute drive from their old house, so he headed straight there. Jas asked where they were going, and he told her they were going to see a potential house. Jas knew they would need more space, especially with Los's two new babies and then Shae's baby. She was adamant about moving out. She didn't care what Devin said. She would not leave her best friend.

When Los and Jas got to the house, they were shocked. They buzzed the iron gates. Outside the gate was a security sector. Once buzzed in, it was still a two-minute drive to the house. It was breathtaking. The house was big as shit, and the lawn was amazing. When you walked into the house, there was a foyer to your left, and when you walked up some more to your right, there was this huge ass kitchen. It had granite countertops, stainless steel appliances, marble floors, and an island. Jas fell in love with the kitchen. Everything she dreamed of was dead happening to her. The realtor told them there were different wings in the house. That threw them for a loop. They were from the PJs. They didn't know shit about a wing.

She showed them the east wing and told them there were four wings in the house just like it. They all had three bedrooms, two bathrooms, plus a half kitchen. If they didn't want to go to the full kitchen, they had refrigerator, cabinet, and microwave in their wings. They were so amazed. It also had an elevator and a panic room. She took them out the back door, and Los almost lost it. They walked dead onto a basketball court. Los was amazed out of this world. To the right, down a walkway, was a big ass pool that went from three feet to thirteen. On the other side of the pool was a Jacuzzi with a cabana. They loved the house. Los told her to draw up the paperwork and do what she needed to do.

This realtor was a beast. She did all the paperwork under an alias and drew up fake business info to match the income. She handed Los two sets of keys and said goodbye. Los called up the moving company. He wanted them in their new home ASAP. He chose the east wing for them since Jas was pregnant. He didn't want her on any steps. He told her to come on so that they could inform everyone before the movers got there in two hours. Luckily for them, it was still early. They made it to the house, and Los told everyone to go ahead and grab their purses and keys. They all got into the Escalade and headed to their new home.

They got to the house, and Los used his keycard. He only needed two because there would be security there by end of day. When they got into the house, Los led everyone to the kitchen. Everyone stood around the kitchen amazed. It was a beautiful sight to see. Los started talking to everyone.

"Aight, y'all. I know this move is sudden, but with me being in the streets and Jas and Shae being pregnant, I felt like we needed to be away from the city. No one is to know where we live, no exceptions. Shae, I already sent Devin the info to here. We got four wings in this house. Me and Jas going to take the bottom east wing. There is an elevator in here for us to get upstairs besides taking the steps. Each wing has three bedrooms, a partial kitchen, and two bathrooms. How do y'all want to do this?" Los ran down everything to them.

Shae said she would take the east top wing. Mrs. Carol said she would take the west bottom wing. They had Jas's two sisters and Mrs. Carol's three grandkids, two boys and one girl. They put the kids in the top west wing. The two boys got one room. Jas's middle sister got her own room, and then the baby sister and Mrs. Carol's granddaughter would share. Now they had to order rush furniture and houseware and get as much as they could today. All the ladies had their own bank accounts and cash. Los told them to order everything that was needed, and he would reimburse them. Jas had the most money, so she ordered big furniture like beds, couches, TVs, and game systems. Shae ordered things like bedding, pots and pans, silverware, towels, and rags. Mrs. Carol always handled food, so she ordered the main kitchen items and then came back and added for all partial kitchens. After they ordered everything, they sat at the only thing that was there, the kitchen table.

Carlos called for security for the post. He already knew who his new security detail would be. After a few hours, there was a buzz at the gate. Los answered, and Devin responded. He also said there were a few trucks behind him. Los buzzed the gate and went outside with his gun in hand. When he saw the names on the truck, he started directing them where to put everything. By 8:00 p.m., everything was put up and made up. Fridges and cabinets were stocked by the ladies, but they were too tired to cook. They ordered pizza for the night. The pizza got there quickly, but Los was too cautious, so he and Devin drove down the driveway to get the pizza. They went back to the house and took the pizza to the living room. That was their first family night, and they enjoyed it. Shae and Jas couldn't wait to experience being moms.

They retired to their wings for the night. They'd all had a long day. They got up the next morning to the buzz of Mrs. Carol over the intercom telling them to come eat. She loved this kitchen. Everyone came to the kitchen, and it smelled so good. She made sunny side up eggs for Devin and omelets and fruit for Shae and Jas. Everyone else had scrambled eggs, sausage, bacon, toast, pancakes, and waffles. The ladies made plates, and they all headed to the living room for a little family time before the men hit the streets. Carlos was finally getting what he wanted. He had his girl, a love child with her, and his street status had changed. What more could he ask for? He knew he had to be on his toes.

CHAPTER 19

Los

Devin told Carlos about the meeting. They rode back to the house in silence. Carlos sent texts to all his lieutenants to hit him on his burner only if there was an emergency. Otherwise, the next few days were all about Jas. He just wanted to rest up. He had that appointment with Jacinda tomorrow. After that, he wasn't coming out until it was time to meet the plug. He was exhausted.

They headed home to the ladies, feeling a weight lifted off them. Their biggest issue was solved. They were hoping for a smooth transition from here. Devin had been giving Los the rundown. With Los having two babies on the way, he didn't need to get caught up in this lifestyle. Los got in the house, and Jas was in the bed reading. She had on a T-shirt and some fuzzy socks. He had to feel her. He walked over to her and took her tablet. He kissed her long and hard. He told her to bend over. She did as he told her. Los spread her ass cheeks and slid his long, thick dick in her. He fucked her with long, deep strokes. He started off slow. He sped up just a little, not wanting to nut just yet.

"Oh shit. Los, baby, I'm cumming!" Jas yelled, not meaning to. Luckily for them, they were the only ones in that wing. Jas was shaking and squirting all over Los. He wasn't ready to cum. He pulled out and caught the rest and sucked her into another orgasm. Jas couldn't take any more. She tried to lie down, but Los wasn't going for it. He went back inside her and fucked her like he was punishing her. He fucked her until he nutted all in her. They laid in the bed, unable to move anywhere. They fell asleep in each other's arms.

Jacinda's appointment was at one. Jas couldn't sleep with the constant ringing of Los's phone. She got up to retrieve it. It was now a little after eleven o'clock. She looked at the caller ID to see Jacinda calling. She thought something was wrong, so she answered while trying to get Los to wake up.

"Hello, Jacinda. Is everything okay?" Jas asked as Los stirred in his sleep.

"Who the fuck is this, and where is my baby daddy?"

Jas looked at the phone like it had two heads. *Who the fuck is she talking to* was running all through Jas's head?

"Umm… Los is sleep, and this is his woman. I'll make sure to tell him to call you!"

"Yeah, bitch. Do that!"

Jacinda then hung up the phone. Jas didn't even let her get to her. She was mad for whatever reason, and she honestly didn't care. Jas put Los's phone on the nightstand to go handle her hygiene. By the time she was finished, Los was getting up. Jas told Los what happened, and he was not pleased. One thing he wasn't going for was anyone disrespecting Jas. He told her he would handle it today. Los handled his hygiene and met Jas in the kitchen. They ate cereal together before he got ready to go to Jacinda's appointment.

When Los got to her appointment, she was standing by the door. She rolled her eyes at him and proceeded in. He wanted to wait until after the appointment to check her about earlier. They proceeded to the doctor's office. He sat while she did her paperwork. When they called her to the back, she was taken in an exam room and given a gown. She pulled her pants and panties down and bent over in her baby daddy's face. His dick was responding, but he wasn't going for it. She then pulled her shirt over her head where her full breast sat with no bra. She looked at Los while she slid the gown on, hoping she could get some when she got out of there. The doctor came in and did the measurements on the baby. She was twelve weeks pregnant. Los knew he would have to prepare for his kids and soon.

Once they were out of the doctor's office, Los walked Jacinda to her car. When they got to her car, he grabbed her by the chin. He started off soft and then squeezed harder.

"Let me tell you something. Don't ever disrespect my woman like that. Do you hear me, bruh?" Jacinda nodded. Her cheeks and chin were hurting. She just wanted him to let go.

"That little stunt of trying to seduce me... don't do it again. I don't want you, bruh. We will talk real soon about your job and shit." He then let her go and walked away, but Jacinda just wanted him even more now.

CHAPTER 20

Devin

Devin went to go see his kids but to no avail. His wife did one of her favorite moves when she got mad. She took his kids and disappeared. He hated when she acted like a fucking brat. He got back into his car and headed home. They had a meeting with James, and he wanted to be well rested. When he got to the house, Shae was on the couch with some ice cream. He walked up to her and took it. He knew she was having a girl. He could tell by the way she was carrying. They had less than a week to find out the sex. He was ready to get his princess's room together. Shae knew that ice cream would have her up all night because the baby would be hyper. She said that was all the baby craved.

Devin sat with Shae and rubbed on her stomach. The baby was kicking like crazy. Devin smiled so wide. He loved that feeling. With his first two kids, he'd missed these moments because he was always in the streets. Every night he came home, he would kiss Shae's stomach and talk to it. He wanted his baby to know his voice. Devin laid his head in Shae's lap and took a well needed nap.

When Devin woke up, it was six o'clock. They were scheduled for an eight o'clock meeting. He sent a text to Los, reminding him about the meeting. He knew Los was in his wing, but he didn't feel like walking to that side. He got up and grabbed a snack. Their meeting was at a restaurant, so he didn't want to eat before then. Devin sat back with Shae and watched a movie until it was time to go. He and Los got into the car and headed to the restaurant. They were escorted to a private room where they were seated. They waited for James to come out the back room. When James sat in front of Carlos, he was shocked but recovered quickly. James finally noticed Carlos, and all his old memories came rushing back to him. James remembered his three daughters that he had to leave. Maybe he was tripping. Maybe this was not who he thought it was. James shook both men's hands and took his seat.

"Devin, who do we have here?"

"This is Carlos, my little homie. He will be taking my place. He is the reason why we been moving so smoothly. It's time I step back. I got a family I need to be there for."

"Hmm. Is that right? Well Carlos… where you from?"

"I'm from the Bricks, here in Jamaica."

"I used to live in the Bricks a very long time ago." James got teary eyed, but he covered it well. He missed his daughters, but it had been a long time since he'd seen them. He didn't want to overstep his boundaries, but he needed to know how they were. He remembered Carlos used to hang around his daughter, Jasmine, a lot.

"Yeah. I remember you. You're Jas's father," Los said to him.

"How is she? What about her sisters? How have they been?"

Devin sat confused. He didn't know James was from the states. He never got personal. Then for Jas to be his daughter... damn.

"Uh... let me call her right quick. Excuse me." Los got up from the table and called Jas. He knew this would piss her off, but he didn't know that was who he was meeting.

Jas answered the phone laughing. All Carlos could think was *good... she is in a good ass mood.*

"Bae, I need you to listen to me. Okay? I don't need you flipping out or stressing my baby. Okay?" Los told Jas.

"Babe, what is wrong? Are you okay? Talk to me, Carlos." Jas was up pacing now, worried.

"Bae, I'm good. Sit your ass down. I know you pacing... But listen. James is here asking questions about you. It's a lot to explain, and I can't do it over the phone. What you want me to tell him? Do you want me to have him come to the house?"

Jas sat there stunned. She's always wondered what she would say or do if James was ever in the same room with her again. She knew the girls needed one parent, but would they be okay with James? Would they accept him?

"Bae, you can tell him to come by the house tomorrow. I just got a headache. I need to lay down."

"Aight, bae. I'll do that, but I'm coming home to lay with you. I love y'all."

"We love you more." They ended the call, and Carlos headed back to the table. He stood over the table and told James.

"I'll text you the address to come sit and talk with your daughters. If you not willing to do right by them, don't come. Jas is pregnant and has been through enough. I need to get home to my girl and baby."

Los walked out of the restaurant with Devin on his heels. He was confused, but he could tell Los had a lot on his mind. He had to, for him to just walk out on a meeting with the connect. Devin hoped that shit didn't backfire on them.

When they got home, Los walked straight to his wing. Devin went to their wing in search of Shae. He found her in bed reading *A Bonafide Hood Love* by Dymond Taylor. She loved her some book baes. Devin was lowkey jealous. He stripped down and took a shower. He got out and put some boxers on. When he got in bed, he told Shae what happened at the meeting. She explained the history behind James leaving, and all he could think was that it was about to be some shit tomorrow. Devin took his ass to bed, preparing for the twisted tornadoes of the pregnant woman.

CHAPTER *21*

Jas

Jas tossed and turned all night. She knew first thing this morning she would have to tell her sisters that James would be coming over. She didn't know what to expect from him. He had not been in their lives, so what did he want from them? Did he have good intentions for wanting to come around? Jas got out the bed where Carlos was sound asleep. She thought that maybe some hot tea would help her get a little more rest. She was going to need all her energy for James's visit. When she got to the kitchen, Mrs. Carol was sitting at the table drinking tea and reading the paper. Jas sat at the table with a worried expression.

"Honey, what's wrong?" Mrs. Carol asked Jas.

"James has resurfaced and wants to meet with me and the girls, so I told Carlos that he can let him come here. Mrs. Carol, I don't know what to think."

"Aww, honey, it's okay to be scared. I think that's a good idea. At least you guys will have one of your parents around, even if you have been doing it all these years. You have to let your sisters make a decision on if they want to be around him or not."

"That is what I was thinking when I invited him, but I don't want them to get hurt like I did growing up. I was devastated when he left. I was a daddy's girl." She was very emotional. Mrs. Carol set the peppermint tea down. It always helped Jas to sleep better. She sat next to Jas and wrapped her arm around her.

"Baby girl, it is okay to cry. Let it out. You have been strong since he left. You have all your emotions bottled up, but I promise a cry once every now again keeps you healthy," Mrs. Carol told Jas. Jas couldn't help but smile. Mrs. Carol was her peace of mind. She loved her like the grandmother she'd never had. Mrs. Carol told Jas to get some rest. She was going to lie down herself for a bit before she had to get up and cook for their soon-to-be house guest.

They heard the doorbell, and it was James. They buzzed him into the gate. Jas and the girls sat in the living room nervously. Jas wanted to see the girls' reactions to him. Carlos came and sat next to Jas and rubbed her stomach. That soothed her a little. James walked in the living room. James, Mrs. Carol, and Shae came in behind them. They all were there for moral support. All the girls just looked at James. Carlos cleared his throat so James could get to the point.

"Hey, girls. I am your father! How have y'all been?"

"More like where you have been?" Jas asked. She wasn't for the bullshit.

"Jas, I prefer we talk about that alone. I would rather discuss that with us."

"Fine. Carlos, come on. Anything you discuss with me will be discussed in front of him."

"I guess that's fine." They went to the dining room. He explained to her about how their lives were in danger because he was a street nigga. He told her he explained it to her mother, and she wasn't having it. She told him to leave them alone. He explained that he didn't want to leave, but for their safety, he had to. He met up with his connect and got a whole new identity. Once they found out who had a hit on him, it was already years later, but he knew Lisa wasn't going to allow him back into their lives.

"Do you know what I went through being with her? She shut down when you left. I was molested as a kid for two years. I took that abuse so that none of them niggas would want to touch my sisters. She died a few months ago." Jas informed James of her life since he'd been gone.

"Damn, baby girl. I'm sorry. If I could change things, I would. Your mother knew how to get in touch with me."

"She didn't tell us anything. Look… what are your intentions? Why are you here?" Jas asked him.

"Well for one, since I don't have no sons, you are next in line to take my spot. I really do miss my daughters. I just want to be in you guys' life. I know it's going to take time, but I'm willing to stay here as long as it takes to build our relationships," James told her.

"Carlos, what do you think?" Carlos nodded his head, and she looked at James. She shook her head okay.

"As far as taking your spot, I can't. I have a baby and my sisters. Maybe you and Carlos or Devin can work something out. I can't do it." James understood totally what she was saying. He wished he'd made those same decisions, but he was only worried about feeding his family. They joined the family back in the living room. They talked about James staying in the house for a while. Mrs. Carol explained to them why it was best for James to stay in her wing. She had more room. On her wing, besides the three bedrooms, she had a big sunroom that could be a bedroom. James had him and his security, so they would be in Mrs. Carol's wing. She showed them where they would be sleeping for the time. Los was glad he'd gotten a bigger house, but he didn't want any more surprise guests. They didn't need it.

They all met up in the dining room for dinner. The men had a meeting on the basketball court. The ladies cleaned up and went into the living room to Netflix and chill. They grabbed ice cream, cookies, and cupcakes. Jas looked at her sisters. They were genuinely happy. After they explained the situation to them in PG-13 terms, they were okay with building with James. With Jas and Shae both being pregnant months apart, they knew they were going to need all hands-on deck.

CHAPTER 22

Shae

A few weeks later...

Shae was in the kitchen trying to sneak some ice cream with extra caramel and chocolate syrup. She was now seven months, and her gender reveal was less than a week away. If Devin caught her eating ice cream at seven in the morning, he would kill her. When the gate buzzer went off, Shae almost jumped out her skin. She looked at the kitchen monitor and saw two kids and a car pulling off. Everyone was now walking toward the kitchen, and Shae knew she was in trouble. Devin was the first to around the corner. Shae's cheeks flushed red. As soon as Devin started in, Carlos caught his attention when he asked why the fuck there two kids at the gate were. Devin stopped short and looked at the screen. Devin instantly buzzed them in. As they were walking in the gate, Devin grabbed Shae's keys off the hook and drove to pick them up to bring them in the house. They had one bag a piece. All he could think was how the fuck had she found him? Once he got the kids to the house, he asked Devin Jr. what happened. Junior gave Devin a letter addressed to him.

Dear Loser,

I done put up with a lot of your bullshit over the years, even up to having two kids that I never even wanted. I was thinking that was gone keep you from straying. Dumb of me, right? Well guess what? Since you want to shack up, now you can raise your kids. I am done. You have been nothing but a fucking headache. I have tried everything to make you do right. See... what you didn't know was I seen you all at Disney World. You thought you was so slick. LOL! Jokes on you. For the past two years, I had my own thing going on. Thanks to you, I am RICH. Thank you. You did something right for once. Don't worry about this bullshit marriage. We never were really married. See I got some secrets of my own, but I'll never tell it. You are dead to me, and so is the damn kids. I never had that mother's love in me, because I never wanted them. I hope you live happily ever after because I'll be long gone by the time you get this letter. Don't worry. I'm not that much of a bitch. There are three accounts set up, two for the kids and one for you. Each account has one million dollars apiece. Good luck, player LMAO! Attached to this letter is custody papers. You have full custody of your children.

Signed, a scorned wife

Everyone was standing around waiting for something to be said. Mrs. Carol knew Devin needed a minute by the look on his face, so she took the kids up to their living quarters. They would order everything the kids needed. Once the kids were gone, Shae walked up to Devin and asked what was wrong? He handed her the letter. All she could say was wow. How could a mother leave her children? That just threw Shae for a loop. She walked up to him and hugged him. He explained to everyone else what the letter said. Los couldn't believe it. All Jas could think was what was wrong with these parents nowadays. He explained he wasn't worried about the money because he had offshore accounts set up for emergencies, and he still had his club and restaurants. It seemed like when they took one step forward, they got knocked back ten steps. Shae sat on the couch ordering all the things the kids would need. They would put bunk beds in the kids' room and a set of bunk beds in their extra room. Shae had less than two months left, so after the gender reveal next week, they were going to start doing the baby's room. Shae was tired of being in the house. She wanted to go out to eat. She decided to go nap and talk the guys into taking them out. Once Shae got up from her nap, she went into the living room. She sat in Devin's lap.

"Let's get out. How about dinner and a movie?" Everyone agreed and got ready. Jas was craving popcorn and seafood, so she was the first one ready to go. It was funny to Los how greedy she was. Shae was out next, snacking on something they couldn't see in her hand. Shae was always eating some weird shit. The kids and Mrs. Carol rode in one truck, and the others rode in a separate truck. They headed to Red Lobster first. They ate in the party room since there were so many of them and then for their safety. After eating dinner, they headed to see a cartoon for the kids. Mrs. Carol took them to their seats. While in line, Los saw Jacinda coming their way. He pulled Jas to the other side of him as she approached.

"Bae, what is wrong?" Jas didn't know what Jacinda looked like, so she was very confused.

"If this bitch tries something, I swear I'll body her," Los said to only Jas. Shae and Devin heard him.

"Hey, baby daddy. What you are doing here?"

"Aye, bro. Get your ass on. For real. I'm enjoying my night with my lady!" He pulled Jas to him and walked to the counter.

"Well make sure you call me tonight, baby daddy. I need some of that dick. Since I'm pregnant and all, I just be craving that dick." Jas was about to beat her ass, but Los gave her that look like he would kill her if she did anything with his seed in her. He didn't give two fucks about Jacinda, but Jas and his unborn were his world already. No one paid attention to Shae. She took off her earrings and jumped on Jacinda. She beat the hell out of that girl. Devin had to yoke her up. She was wilding while she was pregnant. What the fuck was she thinking? Jas and

Shae walked off to the movie theater. Los grabbed their stuff and followed. He told Jacinda if she tried any bullshit, he would make her life hell.

CHAPTER 23

Shae

Two months later...

Shae was due any day now. Her daughter's room was ready, and they were just waiting on their princess. Shae was having real bad high blood pressure due to stress. Devin's daughter was giving her hell. She was one of those neck rolling, eye rolling, hands on her hip little girls. Shae wasn't trying to be her mother, but there were rules that had to be followed. The crazy thing was that she never did it when Devin was home. Shae tried to tell him, but he wouldn't believe her. She was a grown ass woman. Why would she lie on a child? Shae decided today was the day to record this little spawn of Satan. The child was too damn rude.

Shae went into the girls' room. Jas's sisters were with James at the mall. She peeked in and asked Devin's daughter if she was hungry. She ignored Shae like she wasn't even talking to her, so Shae walked further in just to make sure she could record everything.

"Hey. I don't know if you heard me, but I was saying... are you hungry?" Shae asked her.

"Did I answer the first time you asked? Damn."

"Whoa. What is the issue? Since you been here you been acting out, so why?"

"Because I don't like you. You and that dumb baby is the reason my dad left. Then that made my mother leave. I hate you. You're the reason she hates us." Shae felt herself getting angry.

"Let me explain something to you, little girl." Before Shae could finish, she felt a sharp pain and a big gush.

"Uhhhhhhhhhhhh! No! This can't be happening right now." Shae walked to the intercom and hit the emergency button. The bell rang all through the house. The bodyguard on duty ran to the wing where the alarm was going off. He saw Shae squatting. He saw all the fluids and knew what was going on. He called Devin to inform him that Shae was indeed in labor. They met up with Jas and Mrs. Carol at the door. He carried Shae to the Tahoe. They piled in and headed to the hospital. Shae was praying her baby girl didn't come while they were in the car. Shae kept doing her breathing exercises. Jas was talking to Shae's doctor. Devin's daughter just kept staring at Shae, rolling her eyes. Shae told her she had one more time. The tension was thick.

When they arrived at the hospital, the bodyguard double parked and went for help. They wheeled Shae up to labor and delivery, prepping her for the arrival of her baby girl. Devin got there shortly after. Shae's contractions were strong. Once Shae got her epidural, she was calmer and could deal with the contractions. Shae finally got some sleep. Shae was in labor for five hours with her baby girl. Destiny Aaliyah was what they named their daughter. Devin grabbed Shae's phone to take some pics. When he went to the gallery, he saw a video. Shae was sleep, so he turned it down before hitting play. When he saw the video of his daughter, he was furious. She never acted like that around him. Then she called her little sister dumb. What the fuck had gotten into her? He knew Shae kept telling him, but he wasn't hearing her. Damn. Right now, he wanted to enjoy the new addition.

Shae and the baby were discharged a few days later. Everyone was happy for Shae and the baby to be home. Devin went and put all the baby stuff away and to find his daughter. He had to have a serious talk with her. He found her sitting in her room. He walked in and closed the door.

"What's up, daddy's girl? You don't want to see the baby?" Devin asked his daughter.

"No." His daughter was giving him short answers and not looking at him. He knew something was wrong.

"What's wrong, baby girl. Talk to me?" His daughter looked at him and told him how she truly felt.

"Daddy, why did you leave us? Why did Mommy leave us?"

"Baby, I didn't leave. When I came to the house, you all were gone. Your mama took you all from me. I love all of you, baby. You all are my kids; you, your sister, and brother. I wouldn't leave you all for anything. Baby girl, your mom is sick. She had to go away, but you can't blame anyone but her. She made that decision. You understand me? That is no one's fault, and I heard about the way you acted toward Shae. You owe her an apology. Do you hear me?"

Devin put his foot down. He didn't play that disrespect shit at all.

"Yes, sir." They hugged and went to join the rest of the family. Devin sat next to Shae and the baby. His daughter apologized to Shae. She hugged Shae and then kissed the baby. She was so precious. The baby was just sitting there cooing at her big sister. Devin's daughter vowed to love her little sister unconditionally. After the day they'd had, they were ready to retire to bed. Devin and Shae laid down and put the baby in her bassinet. Shae couldn't help but ask what happened with Devin's daughter. He explained to her how she felt, and Shae understood completely. They laid it down until it was time for the baby's feeding. Devin loved the fact that he had the lady he loved and all his kids in one house.

That was a blessing to him. He went to sleep thinking of the investments he would make to secure his family.

CHAPTER 24

Los

A few weeks later…

Jacinda called Los in a panic because she was in labor. He told her to call an ambulance so that she could get to the hospital, but Jacinda wanted to be a problem as always. He told her he was more than an hour away, so she didn't have a choice but to call 911. He was up getting ready when Jas woke up. He told her Jacinda was in labor. Jas rolled her eyes. She was praying this was real. She was fed up with the baby mama drama. She rolled over and laid back down. Los went over to Jas's side of the bed. He kissed her and told her he loved her. She was upset, and he knew that it was her hormones. He was ready for Jacinda to have his son and Jas to have his daughter. Jacinda called back and told him what hospital.

When he finally arrived, she was already ready for labor and delivery. Her contractions were one minute apart. He started recording once the doctor got in between her legs. Twenty minutes later, his son was there and hollering. He cut the cord, and they took him to get cleaned up. Los was over the nurse, snapping away. When the nurse asked what his name was, he said Isaac Carlos.

Jacinda interrupted and said, "No. He is a Junior." That pissed him off. He made it clear that his wife would bear his junior. He just ignored the smug smile Jacinda had. He was pissed, but there was nothing he could do. He sent some pics to Jas so she could see the baby. He then sat holding his son until they were fast asleep. He knew Jas was next to have his baby, and he was ready to meet his daughter. His son was adorable to him. After a few hours, he headed home to get some rest and shower before he came back to see his son. When he got home, Shae and Jas were sitting by the pool. He went over and kissed Jas. She complimented how cute the baby was. He told her how Jacinda waited until yesterday to name the baby Junior. Jas just shook her head. Luckily, she was having a girl, so she didn't have to worry about a boy name.

Jas and Los laid by the pool talking to Shae. Carlos fell asleep right there, holding onto Jas. She woke him up an hour later because his phone was blowing up. He answered without looking. Jacinda was on the phone bitching because Los wasn't back yet. He hung up on her. He told Jas to get dressed. She was going with him. They took a shower together and put on jogging suits. Once ready, they headed to the hospital. When they walked into the hospital room, Jacinda was not happy.

"Are you serious? Who is this, Los? Your sister?"

"Nah. This my fiancée and baby mother! She came to see her stepson."

"Carlos don't play with me. My baby has one mother. She better worries about that bastard she is carrying. The fuck!" Jacinda said to Los.

"Bitch—" Jas said, but Carlos stopped her.

"If you ever call my daughter anything but her name, bitch, I'll gut you like a fish. Don't play with me. You ain't pregnant no more." Jas walked out because she was pissed off. She didn't know why she'd even came. Los came out, and they left together. He would come back when it was time to take them home. Jacinda was discharged a day later. He picked them up and took them home. He had some business to tend to, so he wanted to get them as early as possible. He knew it was going to be an issue with him going over to Jacinda's house to spend time with his son. Once his son was old enough to come out, he would have him on the weekends. He helped her inside with his son. He sat on the couch while she put his belongings away. Once she was done, he kissed his baby boy and headed out.

Every day for the last few weeks, Los had stopped by to check on the baby. Today was no different. Los was bonding with his son. Jacinda asked if he wanted something to drink. Like normal, he said yes. Jacinda made him a drink and slipped a date rape drug in it. She was determined to feel her baby daddy's dick again, and she would do anything to get it. She waited for it to settle. She gave Los the drink and baby bottle. She went to freshen up. When Jacinda was done in the shower. She saw Junior in his bassinet and Los on the couch passed out. Jacinda knew she was going to start some trouble with this one. She walked over to Junior, slid him to the other side of the living room, and turned his lullaby music on.

When she walked over to Los, he was hard as a rock. Her mouth was watering for this sex once more. When she pulled his pants down, his dick sprang to life. She put him in her mouth and took a few pictures. She got on top and started riding Los like her life depended on it. She rode, sucked, and came numerous times all over Los. He came once, but she didn't care about getting pregnant. She knew Los would always take care of them. She recorded and snapped numerous pictures, some of him sleep as well. She pulled Los's clothes back up. She went in his pocket and retrieved his phone. Los would be out for hours. It was time for Jacinda to get her man. She started her picture and text thread to Jasmine. She put his phone on vibrate so she wouldn't wake him. She was going to get the lifestyle she felt like she deserved at any cost. She was all about money and status, and she'd heard Los's name was ringing bells.

CHAPTER 25

Jas

A few weeks after Jacinda had her baby, things were kind of rocky. She called Los for every little thing, and Jas was sick of it. The doctor warned her about stress and her pressure. She was meditating and doing yoga daily for her to keep her stress down. She had a month and a half before she was due.

Jas was lying in bed when her phone started going off.

Hubby: Picture message

Hubby: Picture message

Hubby: Video

Hubby: Picture

Hubby: Picture

Hubby: Picture

Jas looked at the pictures first and thought she was tripping. She had to go look at the number. When she realized it was his number, she tried calling but got no answer. She finally looked at the video, and her stomach did flips. Jas's pressure instantly started to rise. She was pissed. She jumped down off the bed and came down the wrong way. She landed on her knees, and a sharp pain shot through her back. When Jas felt the wetness, she knew she was in labor. Jas tried to get up but couldn't. Jas called Shae and got no answer. She called James, and he answered on the first ring.

"What's up, baby girl?" James sounded sleep. He didn't understand why Jas had called him when he was the next hall away.

"Dad, I'm in labor. Help me. I'm scared. Los isn't answering."

"I'm coming, baby girl. Hold tight." On the intercom, Jas heard James barking orders for the car to be ready and for someone to grab the baby bag. He told Devin to get Los on the phone. James and everyone else rushed in to get Jas out of there.

She didn't want to alarm everyone about the pictures she'd gotten, so she didn't say anything. She was already going into labor early. That alone had her petrified. She texted Los's phone to let him know she was in labor, but she never got a reply. She made it to the hospital quickly. They prepped Jas. They couldn't wait for Los. Because Jas's pressure was so high, they had to get the baby out. Jas was scheduled for an emergency C-section. She wanted Los to be there, but she asked James. She told Shae to look in her and Carlos's texts, and they would know where he was.

When they took Jas to the back, Shae looked at the pictures and videos and told Devin to call that bitch and now. Devin called Jacinda. She answered like shit was cool. He told her she better put Los on the phone and now. She took her time getting him.

Meanwhile in the delivery room…

The doctors were getting worried. The baby's heart rate was slowing. They kept trying to keep Jas calm, but her pressure was still rising. When they got Jas's daughter, Carly, out, the delivery doctor started feeling for the after birth, but what he felt was another baby. How could they have missed that? He started barking orders for them prep on the other baby. Currently, Jas wasn't doing good. She was losing too much blood. They started to lose her. They got both babies out and placed into NICU. Jas had twins, a baby boy and a baby Girl. They had to prep Jas for emergency surgery. Jas flatlined on the table. The doctors put her father out of the room and went to work on her.

Back in the lobby…

Devin had just gotten off the phone with Los, and he was on the way. He didn't sound like himself. When Los got to the hospital, he asked them what was going on. Shae just rolled her eyes at him. She couldn't believe he would do this after all these years. Devin explained what he could as far as they knew. Los sat next to Devin. He was worried. He knew Jas would be pissed, and then after seeing the message thread, he knew some shit was about to pop off. Before he could think any further, James came out in tears. Everyone just stood there and waited for him to say something. When he finally composed himself enough to talk, he told them that Carly was fine. He went on to explain that when the second baby came out, Jas's pressure started dropping because of everything going on with getting baby boy out. He told them she flatlined on the table, and they put him out.

Los broke down. He couldn't raise his babies without his wife. He prayed that if Jas made it, he would marry her and get out of the streets. Shae knew Los was hurting just as much as she was. She got down on the floor with him and cried. Devin tried to get everyone calm until the doctors could tell them something. Shae went and asked the nurse if they could go see the babies. She told them where to go. Everyone went to go see the babies. They were so adorable. Baby boy didn't have a name, so Carlos named him James Carlos. He felt James deserved that for being there when he wasn't. He promised to make this day up for the rest of their life. While visiting the babies, Jas's surgeon came out. He came up to them. He explained that Jas was now stable. He said she was a fighter because she flatlined twice. They gave her pressure medicine and something to make her sleep until it kicked in. Jas Slipped into a coma due to the trauma her body endured during labor. The doctor went out to the waiting room to inform her family. At this point it was up to Jas. Her body needed the rest so they could only really wait and see what would happen.

Jas stayed in a coma for a week. When she woke up, no one was there. She closed her eyes again because all that had happened came rushing back. The nurse rushed in and called for the doctors. They checked her and gave her some ice chips for the soreness in her throat. When Jas's room cleared, Los walked in. She rolled her eyes and asked where her baby was.

Los said, "You mean babies?" Jas looked at him like he was crazy. As soon as Jas was about to comment, in walked the nurse. She walked the baby beds up to Jas's bed. She handed the envelope to Los. Jas was in shock, so Los started to explain. He went and picked up his son.

He told Jas, "This little fellow is who caused all the complications. Jas meet James Carlos. This one here is Carly Miracle, our precious little twins." He handed Jas the envelope that was a drug screen.

"After Shae told me and showed me the messages, I had one done. Jas understand that I will never hurt you. I prayed that if God brought us out of this, I would leave the streets for good. I'm done with the streets. Jas, I want us to get married as soon as you are released. I love you and my kids."

Los got in the bed with Jas and the babies, making sure he was very careful. He had Shae and Mrs. Carol do JC's room. They were only prepared for their daughter, so he had to get everything for his son.

***

Everyone was walking on eggshells after the scare of almost losing Jas. No one knew what to do. She would be discharged soon, and so would their daughter. Baby James had to stay until he was eating on his own. He was only four pounds. He was their miracle. Jas didn't know she was pregnant with him. She loved her little boy. Jas wanted a big family, but after that near-death experience, she was okay with her two and her sisters, plus her god daughter. She had to make sure Los strapped up. She was scared after dying on the table. She couldn't afford to have it happen to her again. The next time she might not make it home to her children.

She was ready for JC to come home so she could have her kids' home with her. She hated to leave her son in that hospital. Jas was packing up everything her and her daughter had in the hospital. She was going to take her baby girl home and spend some time with her until it was time to come spend the night with her son. She was praying after a week that he would be able to come home. It had already been a week, and he was gaining weight. Mrs. Carol was going to keep her daughter while she stayed with JC. They put Jas and the baby in a wheelchair and rolled them out. They got to Los's Lexus, and he put the baby in her car seat. He then helped Jas in. He took them home. Leaving the hospital, Jas was sad. She missed her son already. She didn't want to leave him, but she knew she had to get her daughter home and situated.

When Jas got home, everyone was spread out in the house. Soon as she got to the foyer, Mrs. Carol came to see her grandbaby. These kids had been there for her through a lot and gave her grands a better life. She considered them family. She grabbed the baby and went to the couch. Carlos grabbed all their things and went to put them away. Mrs. Carol sat and cooed at the baby. She just smiled back at Mrs. Carol. That warmed Jas's heart. When the baby started to get fussy, Jas breastfed her. She was so in love with her daughter. She couldn't help but to stare at her baby girl. She was so precious and gorgeous. Los came down and got his baby. She was already his princess. He burped her and laid her on his chest. She went to sleep instantly.

Jas came down three hours later and had to take a few pictures of them. It was too cute. She got the baby out of his arms and went to give her to Mrs. Carol. It was time for her to get back to the hospital. She went and woke Los up. He would kill her if she left him. When they got in the car, his phone started going off. Jacinda had called him five times before she sent a text. Right now, he was enjoying his family. She could wait. The next time she saw him, it wouldn't be pretty. He didn't play about Jas and his kids. He'd almost lost them because of her antics.

Carlos started the car and headed to the hospital. They spent a few hours with their son. The nurses told them a few more days, and he would be able to come home. They went home to their daughter. Jas truly hated leaving her baby but staying in the hospital overnight was not an option.

CHAPTER 26

Shae

Shae got so used to being home with the kids that she stopped her registration for school. If Devin was taking care of her, she didn't care about doing anything but shopping. Since she'd had her baby, the hustler in her just vanished. She became a kept bitch. Shae enjoyed being in the house. Now she didn't even care about the plans her and Devin came up with. He had been so busy helping Los change over that he hadn't even realized that Shae was doing nothing with herself. Her appearance looked a hot damn mess. Shae was used to popping molly and E pills, but once she got pregnant, she cut all the way back. Now her body was craving that high again. She couldn't get either, but when Devin brought home his little stashes for the fiends to try out, Shae would get her a little. Now her body needed more. Shae knew she couldn't go to any of her man's traps, so she decided to find one that was closer to them.

Shae put her daughter down for a nap and ran to tell Mrs. Carol she would be back. She didn't want to tell Jas she was leaving, because then she would want to go. Shae hopped in her car in search of her new favorite place. Shae rode for an hour but didn't have one bit of luck. She did however find something like the hood. There were a group of girls and guys standing on the side of a store. She walked past them to see if any of them would bite the bait. Of course, the youngest one had to try his luck. He looked about seventeen. When Shae came out the store, she started back to the car.

"Aye, ma. What's up?" Shae slowed down so he could walk alongside her.

"What's up?"

"Do you get a man? Shit, you fine. I don't care if you do. Can I get your number?"

"Hmm, if you can help me, then yeah. I can do that?" The boy looked skeptical, but he knew his homies were right there. They were standing on the driver side of Shae's car.

"Can you help me find some nose candy?" Shae looked to make sure no one could hear her.

"What am I getting for it?"

"I got cash for it. What you mean?"

"Nah, ma. You too damn fine. I want you. Fuck that cash." At this point, Shae was desperate for the hit. She asked him where to. The boy took her a block up the road to some run-down houses. Shae knew Devin would be gone for a while, so she knew she was in the clear. They entered the trap house, but the inside was laid. It had furniture, flat screens, and game systems. He led her to a room and closed the door. Shae wanted a hit of the drugs before she went any further. He put a line on the nightstand. Shae took the hit, and the high took her out of this world. Shae felt herself get horny. When Shae looked at this Lil Wayne lookalike, she got instantly wet. The size of his dick was out of this world.

Shae had a sundress on. She spread her legs and started toying with her clit. She felt her orgasm building, but she wanted to see what he felt like. She told him to come get this pussy, and that was music to his ears. He rolled the condom on and stood between her legs. Shawty was extra tight, so he had to take his time. He slid in inch by inch. Once he was in, Shae was enjoying the way he filled her up. Shae fucked him just as hard as he fucked her. She was nearing her peak. Once her legs started shaking, Shae couldn't control it. She squirted all over him. They were so into their sex that they didn't realize two hours had passed. They both were worn out.

At first, the boy thought Shae was just some crackhead, but when inside her, he knew she was new to this. He had to lay the law down. That pussy was now his.

"Aye check this. Anytime you need a hit, just hit my line. I don't want you going to nobody else. That pussy is mine. You hear?" Shae was still riding both highs, and she was loving it. They agreed to get up sometime tomorrow. Shae couldn't believe this little young boy had rocked her world. She was ready to get back up with him. They exchanged contact info and then left. Shae had to feel his lips before they parted, so she grabbed him before leaving out and kissed those sexy ass lips of his. They parted ways. He went to the block, and Shae went home to get cleaned up and nap before Devin got back. Shae took that long ride back. She walked in the house. She got her baby from Mrs. Carol. She put her daughter in her room and went to handle her hygiene. After her shower, she got in bed.

Shae was knocked out for hours. She slept through her daughter crying into the baby monitor. Devin walked in the room and shook Shae. She moaned and groaned then rolled over. Devin kept shaking her until she got up.

"Aye, what the hell wrong with you? You don't hear our daughter crying?" Shae looked at him like he had lost his damn mind.

"You are sitting here waking me up instead of tending to her. Bye, Devin. I am tired."

"Tired! Motherfucker, tired! What the fuck have you done all day? Exactly! Nothing! Get your ass the fuck up and handle my daughter!" Devin yelled in Shae's face. Shae looked at him like she could kill him. Shae went to the other room, grabbed their daughter, laid her in the bed with her, and popped a titty in her mouth. Shae dozed back off while her daughter was nursing. Their baby went back to sleep as well. When Shae finally rolled over again, she was hungry and fiending for a hit of her two favorite drugs. She grabbed her daughter and changed her wet diaper. Shae then laid her between two pillows. She went to their partial kitchen and made her something quick to eat. She laid in the bed texting her new drug. She didn't know where Devin was, but she hoped he stayed out. She didn't want to be bothered with anyone. Shae wished she would've found out earlier that she was pregnant. She wouldn't have kept the baby. She wasn't ready to be a mother. Shae just wanted to be free. Was that too much to ask for?

Shae laid back down and slept the rest of the night. Sometime through the night, Devin came in and grabbed their daughter. He put her in her room and got in bed with Shae. He wrapped her in his arms and dozed off.

CHAPTER 27

Jas

Today was the day Jas bringing her son home, so she wanted to head out to get a few things for his bed and room. He was still fragile, so she just wanted to be cautious. She grabbed her keys and went to Walmart. She walked around shopping for her baby boy. She remembered that she didn't tell anyone she was leaving, so she sent a text to Los, letting him know she would be back shortly. She ran into someone with her cart. When she looked up, it was Jacinda and her two homegirls. Jacinda looked at Jas and smirked. She knew it was going to be some bullshit, so she sent Los her location. She put her phone in her bag, prepared for a fight. Jas wasn't going to wait on Jacinda to swing, so she swung first. She wasn't prepared to get jumped. They jumped Jas for a good five minutes. Jas could only ball up and take the beating. Before Jacinda could get out the store, Carlos and his security were walking in. His security grabbed Jacinda and her two little friends. Carlos had been looking for her. He hadn't seen his son in days. She was avoiding him like the plague.

He walked in the store, looking for his wifey. He saw a big ass commotion and ran over there. When he got to Jas, he was pissed off. He picked her up and carried her out. He told his security to take Jacinda to the trap. He was done playing with her. She was going to pay for everything she'd been doing.

Jas woke up to a beeping noise. Carlos was sitting in the chair holding their son. He was waiting for Mrs. Carol and security to come get their boy. The hospital wanted to keep her for twenty-four-hour observation.

They finally got home to their kids. Jas just wanted to cuddle with her kids and go to sleep. Her face was messed up, and she wasn't feeling it. Her body was hurting. Los told her she needed to put the babies in their rooms and let Mrs. Carol handle them because she was in so much pain. Every time he looked at Jas, he got pissed. Jas listened to Los because she didn't want to cause more pain and strain on herself.

CHAPTER 28

Los

Los knew it was time to go have a chat with his baby mama. She had been doing way too much, and he was tired of her. Los kissed his kids before he left. He didn't plan on being out too late, because he wanted to spend time with Jas. She was feeling insecure because of the bruises on her face. To Los, she was still the prettiest woman in the world. He left and headed to the trap. When he got there, his men were stationed in the kitchen. They followed him down to the basement where the three stooges were being held.

"Uncover her mouth. Jacinda, where is my damn son?"

"Los, please let me go. I'm sorry. I swear I'll leave y'all alone. Just please. I have to take care of our son."

"I know you sorry, baby mama. It's okay. I'll let you go, but where is he? You done kept him from me long enough."

"He is at my house. My homegirl little sister has him."

"Aight, baby mama. I'll let you go… right to hell! Kill them all!" Los ordered his men to kill all of them and make sure they were never found. His men knew that meant chop their asses up and toss them to the bottom of the ocean. Los left the trap and headed straight to Jacinda's crib. Their son together was only about six months. He knocked on Jacinda's door, and a little girl no older than ten answered. Los wished he could go back and make her suffer. He walked in and got his son. He asked the little girl where she stayed. She said next door. He then told her to go home. He grabbed as much of his son's shit as he could and left. There was nothing to look back for. He made sure he had his son's birth certificate as well. Los grabbed some takeout before heading home. He was tired out of his mind.

When he got into the room, Jas was sitting up reading. She loved to read books by Shvonne Latrice. He went over and kissed her. She was so engrossed in her book that she didn't even see Los Jr. When she heard the baby whine, she looked up at them. She was confused, and Carlos knew it.

"Jas, we need to talk."

"Okay. About what, Carlos?" Los knew if she was saying his first name, she wasn't too happy.

"Junior will be living with us from now on. I know we got a lot of new babies here, so what if we get a nanny? That will help everyone out."

"Where is a nanny going to live, Carlos? I don't know about this, and what did you do to his mother?"

"We can put the girls in our spare room and put the nanny in their wing. Our kids sleep in here anyway. That, you don't need to worry about. Just know that she is no longer an issue."

"Carlos, fine. That's cool." Jas was skeptical about having a strange woman in her home, but she did want to go back to school and pursue her career goals. She didn't want them in daycare. She grabbed Junior from his father. She could tell he needed a bath and probably to be fed. She bathed him with some of her kids' things and made him a bottle with cereal, baby food, and formula. She sat in JC's room and fed him. When he was finished, she burped him and laid him next to his baby brother. Junior and JC cuddled up together and were sound asleep. She went to the room. Carlos was lying there in deep thought.

"Carlos, what's wrong?"

"Man, Jas, I love you. To almost lose you in the hospital and to get that 911 text freaked me out. What I'm trying to say is… Jas, will you marry me? I'm not perfect, but you are my soulmate, and I never want to be without you and my kids. I love all of you."

"Yes, baby. I will marry you. Aww." Los and Jas laid there and talked all night. Her body was still messed up, so she couldn't give her fiancé any loving at this time. Los got up and checked on their kids. He then went and sat by the pool to smoke a blunt. Devin was already out there smoking. Los walked up on him.

"What's up, bro?"

"Not shit, man. Aye, Shae don't seem a little off to you?"

"What you mean?"

"Bro, I don't know. She just always antsy and jumpy. Then I know I'm not tripping, but at one point my testers kept getting shorted."

"Nah, bro. You can't be saying what I'm thinking."

"Crazy part is now they be just the way I left it. I don't know. Maybe I'm just tripping."

"Yeah, bro. Maybe… because Shae know better. Ain't no way she would do that bullshit knowing everything that we all worked hard for."

"Yeah. True, so tell me this. Why she always gone?"

"I don't know, bro, but put a detail on her until you feel better about the situation. Just don't cause a problem where it doesn't need to be one."

"Aight. You right, man." They sat out there and smoked and talked for another hour.

CHAPTER 29

Shae

Shae was at the trap getting high and fucking like she didn't have a whole family. Each time she went there, she stayed longer and longer. Tonight, was no different. She didn't have the urge to be around any of the people in the house. Shae could be herself around her newfound drug. Shae was free and didn't have to worry about anything but herself. Shae loved being free. She also knew she would have to go home, or her family would come looking for her. Her new little friend didn't know anything about her life, and that was how she wanted it… no responsibilities and no nigga acting like he was her father instead of her baby daddy. She couldn't stop getting high. Her little friend had left to go and get them some food and drinks. He left an eight ball there, but he told Shae don't touch it. Shae couldn't help herself. She did line after line after line. She was so high that she felt like she was floating. She felt like she was dreaming. She decided she needed to rest. It was time to get her life on track. At times, she knew she was making a big mistake, but she couldn't help it. That was Shae's last thought before she died right there on the floor alone.

CHAPTER 30

Jas

"Hello."

"Yes. This is Brookdale hospital. I am looking for a Jasmine."

"This is she!" Jas was nervous. She knew something was wrong. It had been days since they had been out looking for Shae. She didn't come home after she'd left almost four days ago. Jas was worried.

"Can you come down to the hospital? It is about your sister, Shae."

"Is she okay? We've been looking for her." Jas was putting on clothes as she was talking.

"It'll be better if we talk face to face. Just ask for Nurse Nancy."

"Okay. I am on the way." She sent a text to Los, letting him know that Shae was at Brookdale hospital and that she was headed there. She was furious with Shae. What had she gotten herself into, and why hadn't she called herself?

Jas got to the hospital and waited for the guys. They didn't know what was about to happen, so they just wanted Jas to wait on them so that they could all go in together. When Los and Devin got there, they walked in together. Jas asked for Nurse Nancy. They were escorted to a conference room. When nurse Nancy walked in, she walked up to the table.

"Hello. I'm Jasmine. This is my husband, Carlos, and that is Shae's fiancé. Where is she?"

"Well I'm sorry to inform you guys, but she passed away from an overdose, her and the unborn child."

"What?" Jas was shocked, and then it registered that her best friend was gone. Jas broke down crying. What the hell had Shae been thinking? She was hurt. What would they tell her baby once she got older? Devin was hurt, but he had to ask.

"Is there a way to do a DNA on the baby she was pregnant with?"

Jas looked at him like he was crazy. What the fuck was wrong with him? Los grabbed Jas and walked her out the door before she tore this man a new asshole. He would explain to her later what the situation was.

"Yes. We can. Come back tomorrow, and we can get you set up."

"Okay. Thank you." Everyone rode back to the house in deep thought. Devin loved Shae with everything is his bones. He loved her with all his heart, and now she was gone. She left him to take care of their baby. She wasn't even one yet. What was he going to tell her once she started asking questions? That shit hurt everyone. Now they had to go back and break the news to the kids and Mrs. Carol.

Jas just wanted to go home and lie down. She wished she could start the day over, but she knew that wasn't happening. Jas was hurt. How could Shae leave her in this world alone? She was tired of pain. She was tired of suffering. When would they get their happily ever after?

Jas walked in the door and went right to Mrs. Carol. She sensed something was terribly wrong. Jas explained what happened to Shae, and Jas cried extra hard. Mrs. Carol couldn't hold it. She cried for her baby's soul. She prayed over them all and their house. She held Jasmine until she calmed down. She told her to lie down, and she would make her some soup and tea. Jas was responsible for the funeral arrangements. How did you bury your best friend of ten plus years? Jas laid there crying because of the hurt, but she vowed to find out who Shae was with. Then a thought popped in her head. Where the fuck was Shae's car? She knew Devin and Los kept trackers on their cars.

Jas jumped out the bed and went to the safe. She grabbed her .380. She grabbed the tracking device and put all her stuff in her pocketbook. She threw on a sweat suit and her car keys. She started toward the area where the car was. When she saw her car parked in front of a home, she then investigated the car. A young dude with dreads came out and told her to get away from his car.

"What did you say?"

"I said get the fuck away from my car." Jas sent a 911 text to Los. She then sent her location. He started walking toward her.

"Bitch, can you not hear?"

Jas pulled out her gun. She put it under his chin.

"What the fuck did you do to my sister, bitch? Her motherfucking car is here. Her cell phone is showing this address."

"Man, when I got back, she was like that. Man, I was digging your sister, man." Jas laughed.

"See you in hell, bitch." Jas shot him under the chin. She walked into the house and looked around. She found Shae's belongs in the corner of the room. She grabbed her things and headed out. When Jas walked out, Los was looking at her like she was a different person. They checked dude's pockets and found Shae's keys. Jas got in her car with Los driving. Devin jumped in Shae's car, and security tailed them back to the house. Jas walked into the house, went to her bathroom, and threw up. Los came into the bathroom and hugged her. Jas cried for an hour straight. She didn't give a fuck what her sister had done. That was still her sister. Someone had to pay. Jas loved Shae with her whole heart. Los washed her up and put a shirt on her. He knew the nightmares would come. He knew that for the next few months, he would be playing Dr. Phil. to his wife, but he knew he had to. Jas finally dozed off, and Los tried to get some rest with her. He pulled her close. Jas tossed and turned for a little, but she finally went all the way to sleep.

Burying Shae was the hardest thing Jas had to do. Setting up the funeral arrangements for her and the baby didn't sit right. Shae was supposed to be here right now living the life they'd dreamed of. How could she do this to them? Jas was missing her friend, her sister. She sent Shae home in style. She dressed her in an all-white dress. Her casket was white with gold trimming. Jas sat in the front row with Devin. Their daughter kept reaching out for her. That broke Jas and Devin down even more. They wound up closing the casket so that she would sit through the funeral. After burying Shae, Jas just wasn't up for anything. She just wanted to go home and cry her life away. How did you live without your best friend? Los helped Jas into the limo, and they all went home to get some rest. This had been a long week for them all.

CHAPTER 31

Los

Los finally got around to hiring a nanny. They needed the help and badly. When the nanny got there, he took her to all the areas for the kids. The nanny's name was Dezire. He was hoping having a young nanny wouldn't cause any issues in his household. He'd already had enough for a lifetime. Since Devin had the extra rooms in his wing, they decided to place the nanny in his wing. Devin didn't mind if she stayed out his way and did her job. They purchased a minivan for the nanny to be able to take the kids where they needed. Los introduced the nanny to everyone in the house. The only one that wasn't present was Devin. Since Shae had passed, he'd been in the trap keeping his mind busy. He blamed himself for Shae's decisions. He would have rather he been away from the kids instead of Shae. Now he had to look his baby girl in the face and tell her that her mother killed herself with drugs. That was a hard pill to swallow, but if she ever asked, he would just have to tell her. Crazy part was he didn't even know why she started and what led to the point in her death. Carlos knew it was at this point that they all needed a vacation, so he called a family meeting. They all got downstairs to the sitting room.

"We need a vacation. Everyone is going. Jas, we will be getting married. I need you and my kids to have my last name. Jas, schedule it for tomorrow." Jas got up and went to book the trip. The nanny followed Jas since Mrs. Carol decided to do movies while they got packed. Jas booked the whole first class for their family to be comfortable. Her and the nanny then went to pack all the kids' bags first. They only did necessities; diapers, wipes, bottles, etc. They would get everything else there. They put all the bags outside of the bedrooms so that the men could grab them. They then called the guys to grab the bags. Jas tried to walk around Los, but he had her cornered. She loved her some him. He kept kissing on her, and she was giggling like a schoolgirl. She loved the attention Los was giving her. He knew how to make her fall in love all over again.

Los grabbed the bags to take them downstairs. The only thing everyone had to do was load up. Everyone decided to watch movies until they were ready to call it a night. The next morning, everyone was up and heading out the door. They arrived just in time to board. Jas and the nanny went ahead and got the babies and the kids together. They pulled out the tablets for the older kids. They all boarded their seats to get ready for takeoff. Los sat beside Jas and laid a throw over them. While Los was over there trying to get his freak on, Devin was drowning himself in misery. The nanny looked on, perplexed. Since she started working for them, all he did was come and go or drink. He didn't spend time with any of his kids. She looked at Mrs. Carol, who gave her a warm smile. She got up to go sit with Devin.

"Uh… hey, Devin." Devin just looked at her. He honestly didn't want to be bothered, but he couldn't help but to admire her beauty. She put you in the mind of Megan Good; brown skin, sexy pink lips, short hair… just gorgeous.

"What, man?"

"Don't be rude. Do you not see what you are doing to yourself? What about your kids? They lost their mother. You want to leave them too? They need you. Stop blaming yourself. Take it from a woman who dealt with this situation. I wish someone would've talked to my dad. Just think of that!" She yelled before she got up and walked off. She went back to her seat and started to read her favorite book.

After being on the flight for two hours, everyone was getting restless. They all ate and decided to take some much-needed naps. By the time they started getting up from their naps, the seat belt lights were on. It was time to land.

Everyone headed to the villa. Los already had everything set up for tomorrow. Tonight, was the night they would separate. Mrs. Carol was keeping the kids. The nanny was joining Jas and her sisters. They were so excited for their sister's big day. They all went to their separate villas. The very last villa was the honeymoon. That was where Jas and Los would spend their honeymoon. He had the room laid just for Jasmine. The ladies went to their room to prepare for tomorrow. When they got to their room, there was a knock at the door. Jas opened it and was handed three jewelry boxes.

The waiter said, "Here is your something blue." Jas said thank you and walked in the room. When she opened the three boxes, there was a necklace, earrings, and a tennis bracelet, all with royal blue diamonds. Jas loved it. She went for her phone when there was a knock on the door again. This time, Jas let the nanny answer while she watched her. When Dez opened the door, it was a woman. She walked in with a mermaid cut wedding dress with diamonds outlining certain areas like the neckline and midriff area.

"Here is your something new." The lady winked her eye and walked out. Jas was in love with her dress. Her husband had outdone himself. The next knock came, and it was a ring box. She looked in to see Los's wedding band.

"Your something borrowed." Jas couldn't help herself. She smiled so hard, wanting to go to her husband, but she also knew it was bad luck. She sent a text saying thank you to her soon-to-be husband. She couldn't wait. All the ladies decided to kick back and just relax. Los had them scheduled for a spa night in their villa. They waited. After an hour, their glam team was there to pamper them. They got full body massages, facials, manicures and pedis. Mrs. Carol was also receiving the same treatment. The men decided to take Los out for a night on the town. What would be better than a foreign strip club? Devin was ready to see some new bitches. James and his men were also present. Los didn't give a damn about a stripper. He was ready to meet his wife at the altar. They got a section and ordered some bottles.

"Let's party, fellas." Devin popped a bottle open. Los looked at him and shook his head. He wasn't getting drunk and missing his wife's special day. They had to be on the beach at 5:00 a.m. He wanted to get married while the sun was rising. That was his wife's dream, and he was going to make it happen.

He looked at the time. It was still early. He wanted to be back at the room to rest by 10:00 p.m. His body wasn't used to the time change. Los watched Devin and the guards indulge in the strippers. When one stripper tried to come dance on his lap, he pushed her ass to the floor. He didn't give a damn how bad she was. He knew his wife was crazy. After watching her blow a hole in a nigga over Shae, he knew not to play with her.

James sat beside him cracking up. He knew that look all too well. He used to feel that way about Lisa. No woman could compare, even to this very day. Los shook his head. He was not feeling this. When you finally found a woman that was all for you and loved you with all of her, you didn't do anything to jeopardize that. Some men didn't think before they reacted. Los got up and went to leave. He was going to his room to rest. James went with him. The strip club was not his scene at all. They left everyone partying. When they got back to the villa, James decided to just sit and talk to Los for a few.

"How you are feeling about your big day?" James asked Los.

"I'm ready to marry your daughter. I'm ready to give her the life she deserves. She is the best thing that happened to me in life, and I'll make sure she always has a smile on her face."

"I'm glad you been there for her. We'll see you in the a.m.!"

Both men retired to bed. By 3:30 a.m., it was time to get it. Devin and the bodyguards were just getting back to the room with some chicks. Los walked up to the first female and pushed her all the way back out the door and her friends next. He was pissed.

"Is y'all motherfucking crazy, yo. My wife will body us and them bitches if they look out that damn villa and see them. Hell nah. Get this nigga some damn coffee. You my best friend. Are you crazy?"

Devin broke down. He was happy for his boy, but the pain of Shae being gone was killing him. He had to drink in order to keep from feeling the pain.

"Man, bro, you got to let sis rest, man. She will always be with us, but she gone, man. I know it's only been a few months, but you got to let go. Better yet, you should try and get to know the nanny. She cute." Devin looked at Los and smiled. They all knew Dezire was sexy, but Los was not going to put himself in a position that was going to get him jammed up. After Jacinda, he wasn't stupid. He knew not to let his guard down with a wife like his.

It was time for everyone to get ready. The glam squad was over at Jas's villa, getting her dolled up. The wedding planner who Los hired as soon as they got there to make his wife's dreams come true called for the men to come take their place. The men walked down to the beach barefoot. When Los got close to the water and saw the sheer curtain-like tent, he was in shock. He knew exactly how Jas wanted her wedding, and to see it unfold was remarkable. The wedding planner then called for the kids to take their place. The guards were already at the back door to help her bring the kids down. They put the babies in the cabana chairs. Then they called for the ladies. As the wedding began to unfold, James waited for his daughter to get closer to him so that he could walk her down to Los. First her sisters walked down one by one in their lavender knee-length dresses. Then came Dez. She stood in for Shae. Jas really wished her bestie could've been there with her. Then came James and Jas. When Los spotted Jas, a tear spilled down his eye. To see the love of his life walking toward him made him emotional.

"Who gives this woman away?" the pastor asked as James and his daughters stood next to Jas.

"We do, sir." They all kissed Jas before taking their places. The preacher went through the ceremony until they got down to their vows. Both parties had their own vows to recite. Los began.

"I will take your love to give me hope, give me joy, and make me a better man. I promise to listen, to hear, and to always consider your feelings and thoughts as we travel together on this journey. I vow to love, honor, and cherish you, forsaking all others, as a faithful husband as long as we both shall live." Then Jas recited her vows to Los.

"Carlos, I love you. You are my best friend. Today I give myself to you in marriage. I promise to encourage and inspire you, to laugh with you, and to comfort you in times of sorrow and struggle. I promise to love you in good times and in bad, when life seems easy, and when it seems hard, when our love is simple, and when it is an effort. I promise to cherish you and to always hold you in the highest regard. These things I give to you today, and all the days of our lives." After the couple placed their wedding rings on one another, the preacher continued.

"You may now kiss the bride." They kissed each other, and then they jumped the broom. They all gathered around the table that was set up for their mini reception. They ate dinner while the sun was still rising. There was a cameraman to capture all their best moments. Jas couldn't say she wasn't very much impressed with Los. He'd paid attention to all the late-night talks. He had everything down to a science, and she was very proud. She was now his wife.

Jas stared at Los and then their children. She was looking at a dream come true. They all sat around the table laughing and joking. Jas grabbed the bag from the bodyguard. She walked to the water with the canister that had her mother's ashes. She walked it to the water and tossed them. She knew this would be the perfect time to spread her ashes.

CHAPTER 32

Dezire

Dezire was glad to be included in a special day like this. The lovely couple was heading in for their honeymoon. She grabbed Devin's baby daughter, and his other kids followed. Devin also joined them. It was six in the morning, and everyone was tired. Devin looked hung over. She helped the kids to the room and got them ready for bed. When she was done, she sat next to Devin on the couch.

"Hey. You ok? You look stressed."

"Yeah, just a little hungover."

"Let me get you something for that." Dez got up and got him a ginger ale and some aspirin. They talked for a little, getting to know each other. She avoided asking about Shae, since that was a touchy subject. They had a lot in common. Dez hadn't been with a man in two years. Being so close to a man and having a connection was doing something to her, but she knew he just needed a friend.

"Hey. I am going to catch some zzzzz's. That couch is the worst. You can shower and get in bed with me. It's cool." Devin got off the couch and went to shower. When he got out, he put on some pajama pants and got in bed with Dez. His first instinct was to wrap his arms around her. For the next few hours they slept in peace. That was the first time Devin had slept since Shae had been gone, and it felt damn good. Dez woke up first to the ringing room phone.

"Wake up, sleepy head." Jas's joyful voice came through the line.

"Hey. I'm up now. Do you need me?" Jas couldn't help but laugh.

"No ma'am. We are waking everyone up. We are going to this seafood restaurant in an hour."

"Okay. We will be over shortly." Dez woke up the kids first and got them ready for dinner. She then went and woke up Devin. He was already stirring in his sleep, so she gently tapped him. He opened his eyes slightly.

"Hey. Jas called. We got about thirty minutes to get ready for dinner. The kids are already ready."

"Okay. Thanks. Damn. I haven't slept like that in a minute."

"You needed it!"

Dez started getting ready, and all Devin could do was look at her. She was sexy as hell. They both went to the bathroom and handled their hygiene. Dez slipped on a maxi dress that hugged her curves to a T. Devin dressed down in jeans and a button up. They were out the door in twenty minutes. They met up with the family at the cars, and they piled in. They got to the restaurant and sat at the round table. They decided to do a buffet. They had king crabs, snow crabs, live crabs, shrimp, mussels, clams, scallops, corn, potatoes and more. The ladies made all the men and children's plates and then made their own. They had lost track of time. Everyone sat around talking for so long. Everyone was tipsy. What was a shock to everyone was that Devin wasn't drowning in liquor? He was smiling and laughing. They missed seeing this side of him.

Los paid the tab, and everyone headed back to the villas. They decided to do movie night with the kids, but all the kids wanted to go with Mrs. Carol. She took them to her room. Los and Jas went to their room to keep fucking. They only came out to eat and go back to their room. Devin and Dez went back to their villa since the kids were gone. Dez decided to let loose. Dez grabbed some Henny and a shot glass. They decided to play drunk Uno. After Dez and Devin both had to take five shots a piece, they were very intoxicated. They helped each other to their room. Dez decided to test her luck and kiss Devin. He didn't pull back. He deepened the kiss. Devin took his time feeling all over Dez, but she didn't want to make love. She wanted to be fucked.

"Fuck me, Devin."

"Mmm, I love the way you just said my name. Turnover and arch your back. Let me see that fat ass." Dez turned over and planted her shoulder in the bed and ass in the air. Devin entered her slowly. It took him some time to get in it. There was no stopping him. He beat Dez so good. He had her climbing up the wall. Dez's legs were shaking, and she was squirting everywhere. He wasn't letting up. He kept hammering her spot. She was running like the running man, but Devin had a lot of pent up frustration to let go.

"Uh uh... where you are going?"

"Mmmm, Devin, wait. I'm cumming again." That was music to his ears. He hammered her spot until she squirted so much that he was slipping. It was a wrap. This was now his pussy. He didn't care about anything.

"This my pussy. You know that, right?"

"Yessss, daddy! Fuck me harder! Please!" Devin delivered exactly what she wanted, rough sex. Devin fucked her for hours until their bodies, bed, and floor was soaked.

"Uh… who sleeping in that?"

Devin and Dez laughed hard as hell at the soaked bed. They got in the shower and went to the spare bedroom to lie down. They had a few more days before they returned to life. Devin knew when he touched back down to New York that he was out the streets for good. He wasn't ready for a relationship, but he was digging Dez's vibe all together. They stayed up for an hour just talking about Devin's plans of opening a drug rehab for women with children. Dez was happy about that. She felt it was a good idea. She felt they needed plenty of them. There were so many women with kids who needed rehab and counseling to stay clean. Shit look at Wanda from *Holiday Heart*. She got clean and then went right back leaving her daughter. Dez mentioned the counseling part to Devin. He was digging that.

CHAPTER 33

Los

"Whew… Bae, wait. I got a cramp. Los, please ughhhhhhh!" Los heard everything Jas was saying, but he wasn't letting up. By the time they left for the states, Jas would be pregnant again. He wanted her to have all his kids, and he wasn't letting up.

"Nah. Cum on this dick. You're going to be cumming on this dick for the rest of your life. Get used to it." He slows stroked Jas for a few until he felt her nut building. He started deep stroking her G-spot until he felt her cream all over his dick. He loved the way her nut coated his dick. He gave Jas a break. He went and got them some bottled water. When he came in the room, Jas was trying to go to sleep, but Los was nowhere near done. He grabbed Jas by her legs and dove headfirst into that pussy. He loved the fact that Jas ate hell of strawberries and pineapples. Her pussy juice was sweet to him. He ate her pussy until she clamped her legs around his head. She started shaking. Los got up and entered her slowly. She started shaking even more. He was gloating. He loved making his wife feel good. He fucked her hard until he was nutting all in her pussy. He wasn't pulling out. He laid on top of her and kissed her. He had to stop because he was getting hard. He knew he's worn Jas's little ass out for the night. They spooned and slept for the remainder of the day.

The family got back to the states, and it was crunch time. Los decided to invest in several businesses. He wanted out of the streets. He wanted to be able to watch all his future kids grow up. He didn't want to miss out on anything with his family. Listening to the things that James told him about running to save his family, he didn't want to put his family through any of that. He got his wife and kids situated at home before he went to handle business. He had a financial advisor and a construction team that he and Devin needed to see. They had a few business plans that they were going to put in motion. Los couldn't believe how he'd went from a homeless corner boy with his best friend to the plug's best friend. Now he was the connect. How did you pass down an empire? Who did you pass it to? One thing Los did know was that he would always be the plug. It was just now time to put someone else in the seat. He had a few soldiers in mind, but for now, he would continue to keep his ears and eyes open and stay low. When Los talked with the financial advisor, he made sure to pay attention to what he was telling him. While Devin talked to the advisor, he decided to go talk to his accountant He did some emergency planning. Carlos set up some offshore accounts for each child and his wife. Then he set up one just to be safe. These days, you never knew if the feds were going to come knocking or if the grim reaper was lurking. He'd rather be safe than sorry.

By the time Los was finished with his accountant, Devin was walking out the door. It was time for them to put their creations into work. They met with the construction guys. They had two teams lined up; one team to work on Los's building and the other for Devin. Los wasn't going to stop until all his money went into a project. He put so much negative out that he wanted to finally add some good karma to his life. Los's first project was the boys and girls club. He had numerous adventures in his mind, but coming this way to see the project, he decided a boys and girls club a few buildings down from the rehab would help some of the mothers that were in denial about their habits. His boys and girls club would help him to help a few families a month. He would supply food and school supplies for kids. He also wanted a research room for women to search for jobs and do their resumes. He would have workshopped a few times a month to help them with basic skills.

CHAPTER *34*

Dez

It had been a few months since everyone had been back from Jas and Los's wedding. Things between Devin and Dez had been going well. She'd been helping him to get through the loss of Shae. They still didn't have a title, but they were still fucking like rabbits. Dez was still the nanny for all the kids. She did various activities with them after school. The babies were walking and getting into so much. Dez had a secret of her own, but she didn't know how to tell Devin. They weren't in a relationship, and she couldn't afford to lose the best income she had. She decided to go and talk to Jas first. Dez went to Jas's wing, and all she could hear was Jas's dry heaving. She knocked on the bathroom door before she entered. Jas was sitting on the floor crying.

"What is wrong, pooh?" Dez asked Jas.

"I'm pregnant again. I'm scared after what happened with the twins. I said I wasn't having any more kids. What am I going to do? Los will kill me if I have an abortion." Jas was truly terrified to have more kids because of her fear of dying on the table and leaving her babies without a mother.

"Jas don't talk like that. Every pregnancy is different. You said it yourself. You were so stressed out because of the baby mama drama, but this time, it will be different, and on top of that, you know what to do this time. You will be just fine, love, and you got me to help. Only thing is... I'm pregnant too, so I don't know exactly how much help I can be." Jas knew Dez was nervous because she always rambled on. Jas burst out laughing because Dez was spaced the hell out.

"Dez, calm down, and talk to me. You're nervous, but why? You don't have no kids, and you work for us. We are pregnant at the same time." Jas was tickled because she was starting to feel a lot better after talking to Dez. Over the time of Dez being around, she grew to be a remarkable person. Jas honestly started to feel Dez to be a friend. They got up and went to sit on the couch with some ice cream and enjoy some Netflix. The kids were down for a nap, and the other kids were at school. A little girl time wouldn't hurt. They both decided to send the guys an "I'm pregnant" text. They cracked up because they knew it would be funny to hear their response. Devin told Dez he already knew. He was he was just waiting to see if she was going to tell him. He said that pussy was way more gushy than usual. Los texted and said he was on the way. He knew how Jas felt about having more kids, and he didn't want to force her, so he knew they would have to have a long talk about what they would do.

They sat and laughed and talked until the guys got there. Dez excused herself after telling Los congrats. She checked on the babies and grabbed the extra baby monitor. She went to her and Devin's wing. When she got to their room, Devin was stripped down to his boxers, watching the highlights on the football game. She got in bed with Devin and laid on his chest. He wrapped his arms around Dez before drifting off to sleep. Devin could see them making it real far in life. He loved the bond they were building, and his kids loved her. What more could you ask for? The question now was what did you do with that?

Devin woke up first, so tonight he wanted to do something special to show Dez his appreciation. He called up their chef for special occasions and had him do a dinner for them by the pool. He ordered her some gifts to be delivered right away. He started his hygiene process in the hallway bathroom. He didn't want to wake her before there night was completely set up. After he got dressed, he sprayed some Curve cologne on and then went to get Dez up. He planted soft kisses on her face as she stirred in her sleep. She finally started to open her eyes.

"Get up and get dressed... something simple. Meet me by the pool." He kissed her one more time before he left her to get ready. The bell rang, and he answered it. It was the chef and the delivery person with the gifts. He grabbed the gift and then showed the chef where the kitchen was. The chef always made sure he brought a waiter with him and wine for his clients. He put the wine in the freezer for it to get cold. Devin headed to place the gifts on the table. He sat and smoked to calm his nerves. It had been months since Devin placed a blunt to his lips. As he sat there, Dez appeared at the door. He couldn't help but to admire her glow and to see the beauty of the woman in front of him. He got up to pull her chair out and kissed her before she sat down.

"What is all this?" Dez was shocked to say the least. She'd never seen this side of him.

"I'm showing you my appreciation. You do so much for me and my kids, my baby girl the most. I greatly appreciate you. Tonight, I want to know if you're cool with having my baby."

"I am. I am a little scared because of this being my first child, but I always wanted kids, and I planned on having my child. How do you feel?"

"I'm lowkey excited, but I want to ask you do you want to take us a step forward?"

Before Dez could answer, the waiter came out with the champagne, the appetizers, and a pitcher of water. He placed it down and filled each glass, one water and one champagne.

"Aww, babe. Yes. I'll be your girlfriend, and yes. We are going to have our baby." She got up and kissed him. As they finished off their appetizers, their entrée was coming out the door. When Dez saw her favorite foods, she was overly happy. The baby had her cravings out of this world. Once they were finished with their entrees, Devin decided to give her his gifts before dessert. The first one was a diamond tennis bracelet, some matching earrings, and a diamond chain. The last one was a blueprint. Devin had been thinking about moving into his own house, and now that Dez was pregnant, he knew he had to. He planned to build his home on the same land so that they wouldn't be far from Jas and Los. When Dez's face lit up, he knew he'd made the right decision. Dez was crying happy tears. He explained that it would take them six months to get done, but they would sit down with the kids a few months before they moved. He wanted it done before the new baby came.

They finished off dessert and headed in the house. They grabbed the baby and went back to their room. They laid her in between them and watched movies. They had a good night of just chilling. The twins and Devin's daughter had a birthday coming, so Devin wanted to talk to Los and Jas about one big ass party. Crazy part was that it would just be them. They could invite some of their workers' families and do one big ass park party. He was going to get up with them in the morning. He shot a text to Carlos.

CHAPTER 35

JAS

When they woke up and handled their hygiene, Jas just wasn't feeling good today, but she had some stuff to handle. The twins had a birthday coming up, and she refused to be last minute with things. While she was getting dressed, Los woke up and told her Devin wanted to discuss their birthdays. Jas went to start breakfast. She had an event planner coming in to help her with her kids' birthday. She wanted to do a girls and boys theme, so she was thinking something like a sports and cheerleader party. Los came down to help Jas with breakfast and to steal kisses at the same time. Devin and Dez came down to join them. As they waited on the party planner, they listened to the idea Jas had so far for the party. Devin loved it because all the kids could participate. They were going to dress all the girls as the cheerleaders for the different teams they chose for the boys. The party planner arrived just in time.

Over breakfast, orange juice, and coffee, they all sat and gave the ideas they wanted for the party. They agreed to a block party style party in the park with various bouncy houses, a petting zoo, and rides. They agreed on the date and time. Jas decided to do invites, but they would get back to the invites after Los and Devin got the address to their crews. It was a birthday party and appreciation for the hard work. This was when Los and Devin would promote the one to take their spots. They were ready for this event of the year. They had to get all the kids' outfits custom made. Jas and Los decided they wanted to do the New York Knicks. They agreed to meet in a few hours to head to the mall, but at this point, Jas was horny. She pulled Los all the way to the room. He wasn't used to her aggressive side.

"Bae, what you are doing?"

Jas was on her knees, trying to rip Los's pajama pants. She was craving to suck his dick. Her mouth was watering like crazy. She finally got his pants down and pulled his dick out the slit. She didn't care about his boxers getting wet. Jas deep throated her husband and pulled him all the way out. She kissed the tip and then slid the head in. She vacuums sucked his head until he couldn't take any more. She deep throated him again and this time squeezed her jaw muscles. Los was almost at his peak. Jas couldn't help but to moan. Los wasn't like most men. He was a clean freak. He showered twice a day and ate healthy. She played with his balls, making his nut rise. Los tried to get her off before he came, but Jas wasn't letting up. She sucked him until his nut was completely out and kept sucking. Los's dick was sensitive and tender, but Jas sucked him back to life. Los pulled her up and laid her on the bed. Jas put an arch in her back and waited for him to enter. Instead, she got met with his tongue on her ass hole. Jas 'bout jumped out her skin.

Los got her ass hole nice and wet. He trailed down to her pussy and inserted his tongue in her hot pussy. He placed his thumb in her ass hole. Jas couldn't help it. She was cumming all over Los's face. She was fucking his tongue like it was their last time. After Jas came twice, Los penetrated her. He had to take his time because of how tight she was. He slow stroked her until he felt her walls tighten. He felt the gush of her cumming. He sped up his strokes until she was running. Los wasn't going for that. He pulled her back by her shoulders and held her in place. He pounded her until they both came again. They collapsed on the bed. Jas's hormones had been wearing Los out lately.

Jas was kissing on his chest. He knew if they didn't get up, they would be in that room fucking forever. Los kissed Jas on the lips, and she deepened it. Los picked Jas up and carried her to the shower. They got in, and he fucked her nonstop for an hour until she was shaking and cumming. Los enjoyed when her body reacted to him in that way. Los finally decided to wash them so that they could head to get ready. Devin and Dez were probably waiting on them. When they got to the living room, Dez looked at Jas and bugged the fuck out. They could hear Jas and Los through the monitors. It made Devin and Dez want to go back to their room and fuck. Dez wasn't as horny though. She mainly got sick, so most of their time spent was Devin rubbing and talking to her stomach. She enjoyed the time her and Devin spent because nowadays you never knew when your happy moments would end.

They all headed to the car and left to get their outfits. When they got to the mall, they split up. They grabbed all their shoes and went to order all the custom outfits. They decided to stop and grab some takeout tonight. Jas was too tired to cook, and lately Mrs. Carol wasn't feeling well. Jas reminded Los to have their doctor come look at her. They just wanted to make sure she was okay. Jas didn't want to lose Mrs. Carol as well.

They got back to the house, and the guys unloaded the car. Next week, they had to go and pick up the birthday attire. Jas was super excited to see her babies' faces. They prayed there wouldn't be any bullshit. They put all the party stuff inside of the closet close to the door. They sat down as a family and ate. Dez had a problem feeding Devin's daughter, and Jas had the same issue. The guys took the girls in order to feed them. They didn't have any issues. Mrs. Carol smiled and told them they both were carrying a girl. Jas was confused. Mrs. Carol said pick up your son and watch. Jas picked him up, and he laid on her chest with no problem. To her, that didn't mean anything. Dez did the same, and he did the exact same thing to her. They tried to switch and go get the girls. Dez tried with Jas's daughter, and Jas tried with Devin's daughter. They both had a fit. Los and Devin cracked up, but the girls didn't see shit funny.

"What y'all laughing for? Y'all got to deal with all these girls." Jas was pissed and wanted them to stop laughing. Los tried to hug Jas, but his daughter was not going for it. She kept saying *dada nooooo*. Jas couldn't do anything but laugh. Los had them both spoiled out this world. She was a daddy's girl. She didn't play about him. Jas tried to lean in and kiss Los. His daughter smacked the shit out of Jas. The whole room was very stunned. She was acting out today.

She screamed, "Nooo! My daddy!"

Jas left them alone before she whooped her ass at an early age. Los decided to say something to his daughter.

"No, baby. You can't do that to Mommy." Of course, her spoiled tail started to pout, and he caved as always. Jas decided to go lie down. She was tired out of this world. Dez and the guys helped clean the dining area because Mrs. Carol already went to lie down.

CHAPTER 36

LOS

It was a day away from the babies' birthday party. Jas was making sure everyone was prepared for tomorrow. Just to be on the safe side, they beefed up on security. He got a vest for him and Jas. His family's protection was all that mattered. Jas pulled out Los Jr. and the twins' outfits. Then she got out their outfit. She was ready to take pictures. He hoped things went well. They got in bed so that Jas could be up early enough to oversee the party setup.

***

When they got to the park, everything was starting to look up to the way Jas wanted it. She and Los got out of the car to inspect everything to make sure it was up to their liking. She showed them where to put the cake table, the gift table, and the food table. Most of the tables were in the same area. Jas was already dressed because she knew she wasn't going to make it back home before the party began. The DJ and servers got there at the same time. She showed the DJ where to set up. They had a big grill going, and there was a cook on it. All the sides were spread out and ready for the meal. She had Popeyes chicken catered as well. The bouncy house and the petting zoo were set up. They had a mini train ride. There was a mini basketball goal for the kids. By the time the DJ was spinning, and the food was on and cooking, the kids and guys were there. Dez and Mrs. Carol were behind them.

When the kids saw everything, their little eyes lit up. Jas reached for the twins, and her son ran to her, but her daughter acted like her little ass was PMSing. Jas couldn't wait to have this baby because she was in her feelings on how her daughter was treating her. She let her son down and let him play. The guests started coming slowly. After about an hour, the party was in full swing. Everyone was out enjoying the food and the festivities. Jas was playing with Los Jr. and James. Dez had the two girls, and they were all enjoying their time. Los and Devin were sitting at the table with some of their street soldiers. One of the street soldiers saw the same truck ride around twice. The way the party was set up, you could see the streets perfectly, but they would have a hard time pinpointing because of the activities. He tapped Los so they would be up on what he was looking at. Los went with his gut and went toward his family just in case.

Los told James and the guards to be on standby just in case the same truck came back around. Two of the guards went and pulled the trucks closer to the party. They were bulletproof. When they saw the truck for the fourth time, the window was coming down. Los knew it was going time. Los yelled get down before he opened fire. He let it rip before the shooters in the truck could do anything. Jas was behind the bullet proof tables with the boys, and Dez had the girls. That was the reason they set the party up the way they did. All the women were wedged between the tables and truck. The kids were screaming crying, but the guys weren't letting up until the truck stopped moving. When they got to the street, the truck was gone. Carlos was pissed off. He got his family in the trucks. The guards and some street soldiers loaded everything into it while the others kept lookout for their newfound enemies. The question was who? They didn't have any enemies. Then again, Los hadn't been in the streets, so what did he know? He checked everyone to make sure they weren't hit. Once he knew they were good, he jumped in. He told his soldiers to meet at the trap in an hour and took his family home. Jas was highly pissed, and he knew it. She was quiet the whole ride, holding Los Jr. and James. When they got home, she and Dez took the kids out back. She told the guards to set up everything there. She was going to continue her kids' birthday with or without their father. She was not playing. She walked in to get them in their swimwear. Pool party it was. When she walked in, Los tried to grab her. She stepped back.

"Jas, what the fuck? You act like it's my fault."

"No. What is your fault is that you have a whole family. You been said you was getting out, but no. You still have association with the damn streets."

"I promise on my kids I am getting out, but after I handle this. Any of y'all could have been hit."

"Ugh, bae. I know, and that is what scares me the most. I just want you out. We have more than enough to watch our grandchildren grow." Los hated when Jas got emotional.

"Look… just let me go ahead and get to this meeting. I'll be right back."

"Fine. You got an hour to be back."

"I love you, man. I'll be back. I promise." Los left with Devin. He knew damn well Jas wasn't playing with him. They got to the trap, and Los was now fuming.

"Can someone tell me what the fuck happened? Who the fuck was them niggas?"

One of the street soldiers played a video that caught the license plate. He looked to Devin. He was already texting it over to the guy they used from the police force.

"Do we got beef that I don't know about?"

"We got into it with them southside niggas a few weeks ago, they just mad because we be slanging over there. I told them lay down or get down," one of his many trap boys said.

Devin's and Los's phones went off. Devin told Los they got a location. Los told them to ride out. It was something up with the south trap. They sent a few to sit on the address they got. They were taking out everyone; grandma, sisters, and kids. They didn't give a fuck about Los's wife and kids or anyone in his family, so fuck it. The rest went to check their traps. When they got to the south, their trap was in flames. They knew it was an all-out war. They didn't play about their money. Los had sent a text, telling his soldiers to burn that address, watch it burn, and make sure no one got out. Los was going home to his family before Jas killed him.

CHAPTER 37

JAS

Jas had just finished swimming laps with the kids. She was tired, so she knew they were. She decided to feed them, and then they would do cake and open gifts. As soon as Jas got them seated, Los and Devin were walking in. He sat and ate with them. They all sang happy birthday to the kids. They opened all the gifts from cards, toys, and money. Jas was grateful. She cut everyone some cake. The day was winding down, and she was ready to soak and then get in bed with her husband.

Jas was thinking about getting out of New York. She couldn't do it anymore. Her whole life had been NYC, and she wanted better for her kids. She didn't want them dodging bullets all their life. She wanted peace for her children. She didn't want them going through what her and her sisters went through.

Dez took all Devin's kids to get them ready for bed. Thank God it was the weekend. Jas took her three and got them in bed. She and Los sat with them and watched *Lion King*. This was their favorite cartoon before bed. Jas was so tired. She fell asleep on the chair in Los's arms. He didn't feel like carrying Jas to the room, so he decided to just sleep there with his kids. Dez came in to check on the kids. She didn't know Jas and Los were in there. They all were sleeping peacefully. Dez grabbed the throw blanket and put it over them. They all were so cute. She turned on the night light for the kids and left out.

***

When Jas woke up, she was tightly in Los's arms. He was holding her for dear life. It was Sunday, so she knew he wasn't leaving out today. No matter what was going on in the streets, Los didn't leave on Sundays, so it would be family day anyway. She woke Los up so they could go and get in the bed. Her body was starting to hurt being on the couch. She didn't even mean to fall asleep. Los got up and wrapped his arms around his wife. When they got to the room, Jas just wanted to relax with her husband. She knew after a few hours that her daughter would be up screaming *dada*. That little girl was something else, and Los had his work cut out for him because she was way too much. Los laid down next to Jas and rubbed her stomach. They found out the last appointment that Jas would be having twins again. Jas wasn't about to keep popping out twins for Los's ass. She wanted her figure to stay intact. The first set made her thick, and she loved the weight, but she was not about to be out here looking sloppy. They found out the sex on Monday. Jas was hoping for two boys. They were so much easier to deal with, but she also knew life wasn't going to be that easy.

Jas laid down, and Los gave her a full body massage. Since her feet were swollen, he started with that. It felt so good to Jas. She didn't know what she was going to do. She loved when he massaged her, but every time, it made her so horny. Jas's sex drive was out of this world when pregnant. You would think since Carlos couldn't keep up with her when she was pregnant that he would stop knocking her up. No, not Carlos. He loved seeing her barefoot and pregnant. If it was up to him, he would keep her pregnant. Jas was moaning like she was having sex or something. Carlos was very intrigued. He started to massage up her legs, and Jas couldn't help but to spread them. Los wasn't ready to take it there just yet. He wanted to see how far she would let him massage her without trying to take the dick. He got up to her back side and laid between her legs and massaged it. Jas started to reach for his dick, but he was not making it that easy. He started massaging her stomach and talking to his babies. He massaged her breasts next because she complained about them hurting then massaged her shoulders.

By this time, he was over Jas. While he massaged her head, she quickly pulled his dick out and put it in her mouth. She almost made his knees buckle. Jas was good at sucking his dick. He didn't feel safe the way he was though. She had him in a pushup position. He didn't want to hurt her or the babies. He told Jas to let him stand up, but she wasn't letting up. Los literally had to fall sideways to get out of that position. Jas didn't care. She rolled on top and kept sucking. Jas had her ass in the air, so Los decided it was his turn to play. He stuck two fingers in Jas's ass, and that fucked up her whole suck game. He was not playing fair.

Los had Jas right where he wanted her. He pulled his fingers out and slid right under her. He positioned her right at his dick, but he wouldn't let her sit on it just yet. Los played in Jas's pussy. He took two fingers and slow fucked her until her juices were running down his hand. She was ready to be fucked, but he was not ready yet. Los pulled Jas to sit on his face. She rode him slow for the moment. He knew exactly how to speed her up. He took his two fingers and put them back in her ass. Jas sped up the pace fucking Los's face. She started cumming all over his face, and Los didn't leave one drop untouched.

He finally flipped Jas over and inserted himself into her. He had to make sure he didn't nut just yet. Jas's pussy was still extra tight and wet. The shit drove Los to be premature, and he wasn't having that. He knew he had to just give her deep strokes and not fuck her because she was pregnant. He felt Jas's legs tightening, and then the shakes started. Los stayed on her G spot, so she wouldn't stop cumming. She thought he was done but not at all. Los sped up just a little so that he could get off. Jas kept clenching her pussy muscles, and that sucked the nut right out of Los. He couldn't even pull out. He needed that to release all the day's frustration. They crawled in the bed and went to sleep. They had to get a few good hours before the kids busted in. They had to start locking their room door because they always slept naked.

They got up a few hours later to their kids banging on the door. Los gave Jas her robe and then put his on. He made sure Jas was decent. When he looked at Jas, she was covered. He opened the door for the kids. The boys went straight to their mother, but Los wouldn't let her lift either kid because of the weight. His daughter stood at his side like a little Pitbull. He went and put his boys in the middle of the bed. It was twelve, so he knew Jas was hungry. He went and warmed some of the grilled food up from the birthday party. He put everything on a carry tray and brought it to the bedroom. He sat the kids' food on the floor and sat the tray on the bed. He grabbed the vitamins for Jas to take. He gave her the vitamins, and they all sat as a family and ate leftovers. Jas fell asleep watching TV with the kids. Los couldn't help but to snap pics of his kids and wife. Their daughter was sleep in her food. The boys were engrossed in the TV. They loved action movies. Put some *Transformers* on for them, and they would be perfect angels.

Los cleaned everything up. He put his daughter in the bed and helped the boys to get at the bottom. Thank God for the size bed they had. He cuddled up with his two girls, and they slept like that for a few hours. Los now knew the meaning of family, and he was in love with them all.

CHAPTER 38

DEZ

Today was the day for Dez and Jas's appointment. The guys were going because they wanted to know what they were having. They were praying for boys. They piled into the car and went to Jas's normal doctor. Dez's appointment would take longer than Jas's since this was her first time visiting. They both checked in, and while Jas was called to the back quickly, Dez was still doing paperwork. When she finished handling her paperwork, she sat with Devin. As they waited to be called in, Dutchess walked in with a little boy no older than two, maybe three. She checked in at the desk. Devin wondered where she had disappeared to.

When Dutchess sat down, she looked like she'd seen a ghost. She pulled her son on her lap and gave him her phone. Devin kept looking at the boy. He looked a lot like his kids, but he didn't want to cause any issues at Dez's appointment. They called Dez's name, so they got up. Devin told her to go ahead. He had a call to make. He didn't like lying to her, but he didn't want to cause a problem when this could only be a hunch. Once Dez went to the back, he walked up to Dutchess.

"What's up, D?" Dutchess didn't like the way Devin was staring at her. She knew he had questions.

"Hey, Devin!"

"Who son?"

"Mine."

"Where is his pops? What is his name?"

"Devin, just ask the damn question you really want to ask! Is he yours?"

"Well, is he?"

"Ugh, yes. He is, but I didn't find out I was pregnant until it was too late. I was five months pregnant. I was so stressed over you that I couldn't function. I passed out, and when I went to the hospital, I found out. I been in Atlanta with my mother and sister. I'm only here because my mother got sick. Look… we won't be here long. I promise."

"Bitch, you got life fucked up if you think you going to take my seed back out of NY. I'll body you, so don't try your luck. How old is he? Does he know who I am? What is his name? Man, what is your number? We are going to talk about this shit!"

"Don't talk to me like that. I'm not your little flunky. If you want to spend time with him before we leave, then that is fine. My number is still the same. Excuse me. They are calling his name. It's Kevin."

Devin was pissed beyond belief. How could he have a whole child that he didn't know about? If it wasn't one thing, it was another. That didn't make sense to him. He went to the back and joined Dez. She was already in the examination room. Dez asked if he was okay, and he told her they would talk. After finding out they were having a girl, Devin was ready to cry. What the fuck was he going to do with all these girls?

He helped Dez down to her feet. They walked to the front for her to schedule her next appointment. While they waited on Los and Jas, they talked about Dutchess and his son. He wanted to sit down and have dinner with her. Dez felt it was a great idea. That way, the kids could meet their brother. When Jas and Los got in the car, Devin told them the situation. They agreed with Dez about the dinner. He called up the chef so that he could come cook a special dinner. Jas announced that she was having two more girls. They all laughed because what they were worried about was how they were going to deal with all these little girls.

They got back to the house and went to prepare for their dinner guest. After a few hours, the gate buzzed. Security was asking for clearance on Dutchess. They allowed her in after scanning her car for any other person besides her son. Dez was nervous because now she had to worry about yet another female. Devin saw that look on her face. He walked up to her and kissed her.

"You don't have anything to worry about!"

Even though he assured Dez, the doubt was still there. When Dutchess got to the door, Devin let them in. He closed the door behind them and led them to the sitting room. Devin Jr. stood behind his mama. He didn't like to be around a lot of people and noise. Devin introduced Dutchess first. Then came little man. His oldest two were in shock. Two more siblings? They were glad to be a big brother and sister. The youngest daughter wasn't having it. She jumped on Devin's lap as soon as he sat down. She was spoiled, so he knew she was going to be the one who wouldn't warm up. Devin tried to get her to be nice, but she wasn't going for that. Devin called Junior over to him and put him in his lap. He was starting to warm up to his father. Dutchess showed Junior a picture and explained to her son that he would be visiting his dad that day. She never lied to her son about his father, so he knew who he was.

Junior sat with his head on his father, watching his little sister. She kept rolling her little eyes and sticking her tongue at him. He was very tickled. He just kept laughing at her. Dez tried to grab her so that Devin could get some time in with his boy. Of course, she had a plum fit. Mrs. Carol had to get up and get her because she knew if she tried it with her, Mrs. Carol would spank that little tail of hers. She got down and played with the twins. Junior wanted to get down too. While the kids played, the adults sat around and talked.

CHAPTER 39

DEVIN

"Dutchess, we have to come up with some type of schedule for me to be in my son life."

"I know, but what? It has only been me and him for years. I live fourteen hours away. I am not moving back here," Dutchess replied to Devin.

"Honey, I don't blame you. I want to get the hell out of here too, but somebody glued to this hell hole!" Jas said in agreement with Dutchess. Carlos gave her that death stare, but she didn't care one bit. She meant what she was saying.

"What if he comes and spend birthdays, holidays, and summers with me?"

"I don't know, Devin. We would have to start slow, maybe weekends for now. I can bring him, or you can come get him on Fridays and have him back by Mondays."

"That is a start for now, and we will plan once he gets more comfortable."

"Okay." Everyone got up to go eat. For the rest of the night, everything was smooth for them. He was glad he didn't have to deal with a bitter baby mother. That was the relief he needed. He just wanted to build a bond with his son. He looked at his blended family and knew God had made some tough decisions in his life, but he was grateful. After dinner, everyone went to the sitting room just to talk a little. The kids were getting restless. Jas invited Dutchess and Junior to stay the night since it was getting late. Devin wanted to spend more time with his son, so Dutchess agreed. They set her up in one of the rooms and gave her what she would need for bed. Dez got Devin's kids ready for bed, and Jas got her kids together. The big kids helped as much as they could since Jas and Dez were pregnant. He helped Dez into bed. Lately she'd been feeling pressure. The doctor said it was nothing, but they still wanted to be careful.

Dez wanted to have sex, but Devin was not willing to jeopardize his child's safety. She would have to wait for his daughter to get there. Devin laid next to Dez, but he knew what she was up to, and he was not allowing it. If she wasn't so big, she probably would play with her toys, but because of the pregnancy, a lot of stuff was out the window. She slid her hand down to his penis, but he pulled it back up. Dez was getting mad because she was horny.

"It's because I'm fat... ain't it."

"Man, Dez, go to bed."

"No. You need to tell me why the fuck you won't fucking touch me!"

"Because I'm not about to put my daughter's health in danger. You already feeling pressure. If we fuck, that is more pressure. You only five fucking months. The fuck?"

"Whatever, Devin. Is it your baby mother? I already had to compete with one, so do I have to compete with this one too?"

Dez started crying. Devin hated when she did this. He was worried about only her and his kids. He pulled her close to him, and she laid her head on his chest still weeping.

"Bae, you and my kids is all that matters. Why you tripping? I love you. No one else. Can you just chill before you stress my daughter?"

"Okay. I love you, Devin."

"I love you so much more!"

They cuddled and went to bed. Devin planned to get up and make Dez and the kids' breakfast in bed. He wanted to make her feel better. He kissed the nape of her neck before he dozed off on her.

Devin woke up and got started on breakfast. He made scrambled eggs, bacon, sausage, biscuits, pancakes, cereal, fruit, orange juice, and coffee. He laid the spread out. He woke everyone up. His family sat at the table. Los carried Jas and the kids' food to their wing. They wanted to give them a little privacy. They sat and talked. Dutchess was leaving in a week to go back home. She promised that Junior could come back only if he was okay with staying with his father one day during the week without her. Devin insisted to do it today since she needed a break. He booked her a spa day just to ease her mind. Junior ran off with the kids after breakfast.

Dez decided to go lie down. The baby was wearing her down. Dez waddled her way to the bedroom. After Dutchess left junior, Devin checked in on them all. When he saw they were fine, he went to lie down with Dez. He wasn't tired, but he needed to just relax. They laid around for a while before Devin went to check on the kids. They were all asleep on the floor. Devin picked them up one by one and laid them in their beds. He wished he could have all the kids in one house, but he'd just have to settle for the visit. He was going to set up an account to put money in for him each month so that Dutchess could take care of his seed.

CHAPTER 40

JAS

A few months later…

It was time for Jas's babies. Today she was being induced. Dez had her daughter last night at midnight. Jas was ready for these little girls to get out of her body. She was ready to be one person again. She was just praying for a safe delivery this time. She had Carlos in the room with her. Mrs. Carol and James had the kids at the house since they were too young to be in the hospital. Jas really wanted to try a water birth, but one baby was breached and wouldn't come out. Jas knew her daughters were going to be stubborn like their damn daddy.

They rolled Jas to the surgery room. They gave her the medicine she needed for the pain. She prayed that if she had any more kids, it would only be one next time. They cut Jas in the same incision as before. Los was excited to see the birth of his daughters. He had the camera rolling. They pulled the first baby out. She was six pounds and four ounces. She was the lighter baby. The breached baby was putting up a fight. She wasn't trying to come out just yet. When they pulled her out very carefully, she came out four pounds and three ounces. She was the darker baby. Los couldn't wait for them to get their features.

The doctors went and closed Jas back up. She slept through the process, but because of the last time, they kept checking her vitals. Jas was doing great. They took the babies to get tested. They told Carlos to get cleaned up and meet them in labor and delivery. Jas was put in her room. Los was happy his girls were finally here. That was a joy to see. They had three days left to be at the hospital before they could bring their babies home. Los sent pics to the family. Devin and Dez were scheduled to move into their house this week. While Dez was in the hospital, he was working extra hard to get the furniture and everything else moved in. She came home the day before Jas. Los had James rearranging the bedrooms and wings. Now that Devin and Dez were moving, their wings were empty. James and his security had one wing upstairs. Mrs. Carol had the opposite wing upstairs with the elevator. Her grandkids now had their own room in her wing. Jas and all the kids had the downstairs wing. Her sisters had two of those bedrooms. Los was glad that everyone was comfortable. They had all the babies' rooms redone before Jas got too far in her pregnancy.

After a few days in the hospital, it was time for Jas to go home with her babies. Talk about excited to leave the hospital! She was tired of being woken up, pinched, and poked. She just wanted to get on a sleep schedule with the twins. Jas also had to prepare for the online classes she would be starting in a month. She was not joking when she said she wanted a better life for her children. She didn't see how some females sat back and let a man take care of them. No offense to her husband, but all men had dog tendencies. You never knew if he was going to get that urge to creep around or fuck off period. Then you'd be stuck looking crazy because this man took care of you. Not Jas!

She didn't care how long they'd known each other. She was always prepared. Jas loved her husband dearly, but he had always been a ladies' man. Jas got home and got settled in with their twin daughters. They were good babies and only cried when hungry or wet. She didn't want anyone holding and spoiling them, Los included. She needed them to stay content.

After a few weeks of being home, Jas had the girls on a great sleep pattern. They only woke up every four hours. That gave her time to do everything she needed like studying and tending to the other children. Most times, her sisters would keep an eye on the other twins. Sometimes, she would let them come lay with her. She didn't want them to feel neglected in any way. She loved going to school. It gave her something to look forward to.

Chapter 41

Los

Los and Devin's first construction projects were now done. Los was excited to open his boys and girls club. He had so much riding on this project, and it was finally finished. The boys and girls were a program that the kids could come to year around. They could get homework help, tutoring, and play all types of activities. They had a van that would pick the kids up from school and take them home. Carlos was working on getting a few different teams started for some AAU. He also was going to have a few cheerleading squads. He did not want to leave any kids out. He also had another part that was a daycare. He wanted to give as much help as possible to his old community. Since Carlos and Devin were fully out of the streets, all they had was their projects to keep them busy. Devin had been interviewing and running background and street checks on all staff. Once he got the perfect staff, he was now ready to start setting everything up. He bought ten fifteen-passenger vans. He stocked all the kitchens with the food and drinks the kids would need.

Today was the day for grand opening. Today was the day to sign up for all programs. The turnout was unreal. You had parents and kids everywhere. A few dope boys came through with donations. Los was very proud of his accomplishment. To have his wife right next to him voicing how proud of him she was, Los couldn't wait 'til the day his boys could come play sports. Jas wanted to help around the center, so she enrolled all the kids in the daycare program. Between studying and classes, she was going to work with cheerleading and tutoring. Her sisters also volunteered to be tutors as well. Dez and Devin couldn't help, because Shae's Rehab would be opening next week. He too added some good assets to his program that would benefit the community. They were all about giving back.

They told all drug dealers to keep the drugs away from their vicinity. They all knew just because Los and Devin were out the street didn't mean they weren't still about their gun play. Their respect in the streets tripled just because of what they were doing for the community. Los also had James use some of his connects to schedule big time stars to come and check out the kids or perform for their concerts. Los wanted to make a big difference in his community. The mayor even stopped by to see what all the talk was about.

When he saw what Los was doing, he gave Los a plaque. The mayor said not too many people would do something like this to help the community. Los felt good to be doing for the community. He got out there and helped coach the little boys' league for the day. Jas watched them try to teach the little girls cheerleading routines. They were making it way more complicated, so Jas got out there and helped. She broke the girls into groups. She started with the youngest ones. They were the hardest to learn it. After working with them, Jas was all out tired. She looked at Los, and he was having a blast. She decided to just go to the kitchen and grab her some to drinks. It had been a while since she'd gotten active like that.

Jas was tired, so she decided to go to Los's office and nap. She checked on her kids before going to his office. She got on his couch and went straight to sleep. She woke up to soft kisses. She opened her eyes to her husband. He was all sweaty and looking so good. She kissed him back. She climbed on top of her husband. It had been a while since they had time to be together intimately. Jas kissed him with so much passion "Get undress!" Los told her while he went to lock the door. when he came back over to the couch and laid her down, then he kissed her feet and then up her legs. When he got to her pearl, he gave her soft kisses. He then nibbled on her clit. After nibbling, he started to suck her clit. Jas tried to run, but she was wedged between Los and the couch. He had her folded like a pretzel. He was sucking on her clit like it was a pacifier. Jas was shaking and cumming. Los stuck two fingers into Jas's pussy. He felt her pussy muscles clenching. Once Jas came, Los penetrated her. It had been so long. He had been craving his wife.

Los slow stroked her for a while just so the rest of her nut could come out. Once she was off that wave, it was time to put her on another one. He went deeper and faster, asking her whose pussy was it. Los tried to keep their voices to a minimum, but they were way too into it. Jas was shaking and cumming, but he was not done with her. He flipped Jas over the edge of the couch and went deep. Jas was hanging over the couch, biting the arm. Los was giving her the business, and her legs had yet to stop shaking. She was on orgasm three. This was exactly why Jas stayed pregnant.

Jas started throwing it back. She let Los have his fun, but now it was her turn. Jas arched her back and fucked Los back. He couldn't handle Jas's backshot or when she rode him. As Jas was throwing it back, Los was enjoying the ride, but he knew Jas was going to cum first. He felt his favorite gush and knew she was on number four. He pulled her up and let her ride him. He knew she was tired. Jas slow rode him for a few minutes, trying to get her body under control. Once Jas was rejuvenated, she got in a squat position and bounced her ass up and down. Los knew he was not going to be able to last long. If Jas didn't want to get pregnant, she'd better watch out. Los got close to his peak, so he flipped her onto her stomach and drilled her little ass. She knew Los was about to cum, so she just laid with her ass in the air.

Once her juices were trickling down his shaft, he could not hold it any longer. When his nut got to the head, he quickly pulled out and shot his seeds on his wife's ass. He told her stay there so he could clean her up. He went to the bathroom in his office. He got some paper towels and wiped his wife off. He helped her up. They both got dressed and fixed themselves up. Los knew it was time to get Jas home because once she got tired, she got grumpy.

They grabbed their kids to go home. Los wanted a little more of his wife, but he knew his kids were not going for it. They were some cock blockers. Those were his kids though, and he loved them.

Los couldn't believe the steps he was now taking. It was no longer just about him but about his family. He never thought he would be there. Shit was crazy.

They got home with their babies and took them to their room. Jas got them ready for dinner. They were eating pizza. After dinner, they laid with them until they dozed off during their favorite movie. Once the kids were sleep, Los and Jas retired to their room. Who would've thought their life would consist of five kids. Even though junior was not Jas's biological son, you could not tell her that Los Jr. was not her son. Jas had big dreams for her family, and she was almost there. A few more months of school, and she was done.

JAS

Los and Jas were now married with five kids. Their twins were now five years old. Their twin daughters were three years old. Carlos Jr. was turning six this year. Jas was a successful college student. She was in her last year to become a case manager. Jas's goal was to help youth who couldn't help themselves and those in bad homes with mothers and fathers who suffered from addiction, whether it may be alcoholism, gambling, or drugs. She wanted to keep as many kids safe as she possibly could. That was what her life was set out to be. Her sisters were doing great. They all had a great bond with James who decided to stay in the states to be there for his daughters and his grandsons and granddaughters. He promised to keep them safe at all costs.

James Carlos and Carly Miracle were the splitting images of Carlos. They also had custody of Carlos Jr. who was Jacinda's son. They had two more kids, twin girls who they named Shae and Elizabeth. They are now three-year-old. They didn't need any more kids at this point. They still had a house full, except now their house consisted of them and their kids and Mrs. Carol and her grands. Life had been great to this couple, and all they could do was think back on all the things they went through just to get to the point of being with the ones they loved.

Jas never thought she and Carlos would be there with kids. It damn sure wasn't easy, but it was worth it. These past few years had been hard on everyone. Jas really missed her friend. She never thought Shae would resort to that lifestyle. Jas always wondered what Shae was thinking. She knew her best friend, and she was a strong ass female, but sometimes life could take you by storm, and if you weren't strong enough, then it could knock you down.

Shae missed so much in her daughter life. It was crazy but No matter what, Jas always told her about Shae and showed her pictures. She used to blame Devin for Shae's overdose, but she eventually realized he was hurting just as much. He was raising all his kids without their mothers. Jas was glad she never let the stress of Carlos's street life push her to be another victim to the streets. After losing Lisa and then Shae, it took a lot out of Jas. All she could do was blame herself because she couldn't help them, more so Shae because they lived together for so long.

Jas just recently found out she was pregnant again. She was okay with having another baby because all her kids were older, but after that, Jas did not want any more. Jas wanted to plan a surprise dinner to tell Los about the new baby. Devin was proposing to Dezire, so they planned to make it a double surprise. Jas was nervous about this baby after what had happened on the delivery table last time. No matter how many pregnancies she had, she always had that nervous feeling. She had been going through counseling to help her get through everything that she had been through. From being molested at a young age to raising her sisters and then losing her best friend and dying in the middle of birth, the only thing she couldn't disclose was her murdering the guy she blamed for Jas's overdose.

She had a strong feeling that this time would be smooth. She was Los's only woman besides their daughters. He knew if he did anything dumb or stupid, she would cut his dick off and feed it to him. Mrs. Carol was a God send. She had been in all their lives through it all, and they owed her their lives, so they decided to send Mrs. Carol on a cruise of her decision for eight days and seven nights. The kids were probably going to lose their life without Mrs. Carol, but she needed the break.

They sent her off to Jamaica. She had one bodyguard with her for safety reasons. She had been there for them every step of the way, and it was only right. Her grandkids looked up to Jas and Los because they took them from the projects and gave them a home. Their parents also left them at a young age. Same way Mrs. Carol helped with Jas and Los's children; they helped her grands. They bought them clothes and shoes for school and helped with homework. Jas was very proud of Los and his accomplishments. He gave a lot back to the community.

Devin

He now had the hottest strip club in the city. He also owned the hottest night club. He had a chain of restaurants now. Devin would have never thought he would be married again with more kids. Their kids were one, three, five, six, twelve, and thirteen. What was Devin going to do with three girls? They were some feisty little girls, but he had them extra spoiled. He loved all his kids dearly. Dez was the proud owner of a nail salon and a hair salon. She owned them and had a manager to manage them. Devin couldn't believe after everything that him and Dez worked so hard together to get all these business. He still blamed himself for not pushing Shae to do something to better her life. He was so busy trying to convert to a businessman instead of a street nigga that he missed the signs.

Devin had a house built beside Los and Jas's house. They needed their space. There were too many kids being produced, but Devin wouldn't change any of life's events except Shae's overdose. He missed her a lot, and he would never forget her, especially since his daughter looked just like her. They all had their ups and downs, but they made it through together. It took his kids a while getting used to the nanny being Devin's new woman. This time around, he knew he'd made the right decision. He loved his girl and kids dearly. Devin was completely out the drug game and had invested money in a little bit of everything. He went through a lot with trying to get his kids in a better head space once they realized their mother was gone for good. They finally adjusted to it, and now everything was going as he'd hoped.

He opened Shae's Rehab a year after Los and Jas's wedding, and he was truly happy about that. It was a big help to a lot of women. He planned on branching off and opening two more in a different area. Devin now knew that Shae was in a better place and looking over him and his daughter. She was now three years old, and she called Dez mommy. There was no point in changing that.

He first talked to Jas about it because he didn't know how to take it. Jas explained to him it was natural for a child to call another adult who was present in their life Mommy or Daddy. She explained it was okay if he decided to one day marry her. He then knew his decision. His kids loved Dez. She was the mother figure and woman they all needed. She came and changed his whole life.

Dutchess let Junior come to their home a lot more since they moved out of the city. They had managers for everything, and from time to time they went up there and watched things run just to ensure there were no issues. Devin's life would be complete once he made Dez his Mrs.

Dez

It had been an up and down roller coaster for Dez, especially around the times that Shae's birthday or death day came around. It was like Devin got into this funk, and all the children saw it. Her two babies were attached to their daddy. Dez had a daughter who was now three and a son who had just turned one. She hated when he went back into that shutting down stage, but what exactly could she do? You know men. They knew it all, so how could you explain it to him? Dez made herself a promise that if he didn't get it together, she was leaving, and she was taking all the kids.

Over the past three years, the kids really took to Dez. She loved those kids like they were her own. What more could she ask for? Her life was simply perfect, but Devin just wouldn't let go of Shae. How could you compete with a ghost? Shit would give you the chills even thinking about it. Overall, Dez was now running the rehab for Devin. She added a little to the rehab to help the women out. Besides the rehab, they had a spa and a makeover area. After they completed the program, they gave them a full makeover and helped them get jobs. She loved what she was doing to help. It was hard at first because of her past with her mother and her addiction. This helped her to get over some of her past issues to hear the women speak on why they did drugs and what made them resort to it in the first place. They explained why they couldn't get off the drugs no matter how hard they tried. So far, they'd helped a few hundred people in a few years. They made them come back and update. They also gave the homeless women a place to live. She was truly happy for the difference they made. She couldn't ask for a better life.

She raised her kids and still managed her business. She was thankful that Devin built her the business. It gave her something to do outside of the kids. Devin was ready for more, but Dez was not having it. While he was gone from the hospital, she had them insert a Mirena. She was not going to be popping out babies like Jas. No sir! Her body didn't even fully bounce back from their daughter, but she worked the weight into the right places. She didn't want Devin to become unattracted to her, so she did everything possible to stay in shape.

Carlos

Being a married man had its perks for Carlos. He loved going home to his family after a hard day of work. Carlos was now the proud owner of a rec center, a daycare, and two restaurants. Mama Carol ran both restaurants for him. His next developing project was almost done. Once the inspectors came today, he would be ready to open. He couldn't wait to see his wife's face. Today was the day his wife would see her new office. He paid to open her own children's outreach. She almost got her social service degree, and he wanted her to have that one thing she wanted so badly. His wife was his world, and he planned to give her the world back.

He loved his wife with all of him. Los sent a check to Dionne's baby mama to help with taking care of the kids. She finally resurfaced after a few years. She now resided back in the projects. Even though what Dionne did was fucked up, Los still looked out on the strength of the kids. He didn't want Dionne's son to grow up grimy like his pops, so he tried to help them get out of poverty.

The night of...

Carlos had his wife blindfolded as they pulled up the center. They pulled up, and he helped his wife out. He walked her up to the door and pushed the door open. When he walked her inside, the lights were off. He took the blindfold off, and when he did, everyone yelled surprise! Jas was really confused because she didn't see the outside. She looked to Los and asked what it was. He took her back outside and uncovered the sign. When she saw the sign said Lisa's Place, Jas broke down. She knew exactly what it was.

Jas gave Los the gift box. When he opened the box, he about lost it. He wanted another baby so bad, and he finally popped one in her. He was excited. Devin finally got up the nerve to propose. Devin got down on one knee and asked her to be his wife. She said yes. Dez was excited to be Devin's wife. She was happy he'd finally came to and realized the woman he had in her. She kissed Devin passionately. All she could think was *Lord, don't let me get pregnant again.* They enjoyed the rest of their night with their family and a few friends. Who would've thought these couples would get to where they were today? It was a long journey, but they loved it.

Los finally got Jas a house outside of the city. They moved to Staten Island. That way they could still be close to their businesses. He presented that present to her as well. Jas was jumping around with excitement. She was finally getting her kids away from the city. She wished it would have been sooner, but better late than never. That was the reason Jas loved her husband so much. He knew exactly how to make her happy. Happy wife equaled a happy life. Carlos could tell his wife was enjoying herself, but he could tell the emptiness of Shae not being around was really weighing on Jaz. With Shae's birthday coming up, he had his work cut out for him.

The end.

CPSIA information can be obtained
at www.ICGtesting.com
Printed in the USA
LVHW061716230819
628745LV00008B/271/P

9 781088 940037